The Fantods of Risk

Also By H. Felix Kloman

Mumpsimus Revisited: Essays in Risk Management

The Fantods of Risk

Essays on Risk Management

For Cis –
who has seen it all!

Flix

H. Felix Kloman

ISBN: Hardcover 978-1-4363-0227-2
Softcover 978-1-4363-0226-5

This book was printed in the United States of America.

Published by Seawrack Press, Inc., 61 Ely's Ferry Road, Lyme, Connecticut 06371-3408, USA (www.seawrackpress.com)

To order additional copies of this book, contact:
Xlibris Corporation
1-888-795-4274
www.Xlibris.com
Orders@Xlibris.com
45230

CONTENTS

Foreword 9

Chapter 1 Preliminary Conclusion: What *Is* Risk Management? 11

Chapter 2 Things That Go Bump in the Night 16
- Things That Go Bump in the Night 16
- London: July 7, 2005 21
- "The earth is a twitchy system." 22

Chapter 3 *Katrina* and What It Can Tell Us 25
- Katrina and Evacuation 25
- Katrina Again 27
- Lessons from Katrina 33

Chapter 4 Risk and Reputation 35

Chapter 5 Population, Fundamentalism and Climate Change 41
- The Frog and Boiling Water 41
- Issues in Uncertainty 42

Chapter 6 Gambling and Litigation: A Connection? 48

Chapter 7 A Contrarian's View of Insurance 51
- 1994 Paper: A Contrarian's View 51
- 2005 Paper: Is Anyone Listening? 58
- 2007 Paper: Deaf Ears and No Voices 60

Chapter 8 Don't Step on the Tail of a Tigress! 63
- The Tigress: Is She Different? 63
- Sense of the Ridiculous 66

Chapter 9 The Nature of Risk and Fear 67
- Fear and the Future 67
- What Exactly is Risk? 70

Risk, Plus and Minus 72
Why, Oh Why? 73
The Crippling Effects of Fear 74
The Uncertainty Principle 77
Financial Risk Management 78

Chapter 10 Ideas and Global Risks 81
Peter Bernstein's Big Ideas 81
Lessons from Denmark and China 82
The Grasshopper versus Chicken Little: Avian Flu 84
On Transparency 85

Chapter 11 Executive Compensation and Apologies 87
Excessive Executive Compensation 87
More on Reputation and Executive Compensation 90
Update on Apologies 92

Chapter 12 The Fox and the Hedgehog 94

Chapter 13 Some Musings on Risk Management 100

Chapter 14 Does Risk Matter? 105
Does Risk Matter? 105
Four Times Three 107

Chapter 15 Risk Management and Monty Python 113

Chapter 16 Introduction: The Future of Risk Management, Again 123

Appendix 1 A Risk Management Reading List 131

Dedication

To my wife Ann, for whom risk management remains a mystery

FOREWORD

Is repetition a failure or a necessity? This book is my personal testimony to repetition as a requirement to implant new ideas on smug memories excessively protected by the past and tradition. It is also an expression of my recurring fantods about the nature of risk (a fantod is a "state of extreme nervousness, restlessness, or irritability"). I'm not yet sure what it all means and therefore continue in my state of restless curiosity! These essays include articles that I wrote over a span of twenty years, from 1988 through 2007, most from the pages of *Risk Management Reports,* the bi-monthly and then monthly commentary of which I was founder, publisher, editor and principal writer for thirty-three years and three months, to March 2007, when I passed the baton of leadership to a new, younger, more agile, and enthusiastic editor. They are essays in humility. I learned early on that trying to create an entirely new comment each issue left important ideas unfulfilled in the minds of my readers. They, and I, both wanted restatements of major thoughts, analyses from new angles, to test and improve them. Thus I often found myself repeating earlier insights, using different vantage points and illustrations. This approach is common in music, when composers take a familiar theme and treat it to numerous variations, all of which serve to implant the basic idea more firmly in the minds of listeners.

So I make no apology whatsoever for the repetition of familiar ideas in these pages: it is necessary to help persuade readers as well as to convince myself of their validity. Ideas unrepeated are ideas that I have discarded over time and study. Yet I remain restless and often unconvinced of what I am saying.

Risk Management Reports started in January 1974, when, as senior partner of Risk Planning Group, Inc., a four-year-old risk management consultancy, I spun out the first *RMR*. I wanted, as I stated then, "to bridge the theoretical and the pragmatic, from design to implementation" in risk management. The issues appeared bimonthly, featuring a short section called *Current Comment* that I wrote, along with a longer monograph, some from me but most from others. My first *Comment* included several technical insurance topics (market conditions, workers' compensation reforms, fire protection, a product safety film), in keeping with the initial work of my consulting firm, but I also commented on the importance of corporate community responsibility, citing a new policy from Chicago's Continental Illinois Bank. The monograph itself, on "Risk Management: Europe and the United Kingdom," illustrated my global focus that continues to this day,

Twenty years later, in January 1994, I converted *RMR* to a monthly format, "shorter and more provocative," as I wrote, intended to focus on "building connections among those of us who practice and teach risk management today." My comment then is as applicable as it is today: "I have argued and cajoled, sometimes not as persuasively as I would have liked, that risk management is a multi-disciplinary approach to dealing with the uncertainties of modern living."

This book, then, is both a valediction and a commencement, after some 336 consecutive issues. It starts with my "preliminary conclusion" about the nature of risk and its management in organizations, stressing how much I really do not know about this discipline. It continues my restlessness, my fantods, about the discipline. And it ends, properly, with a tentative "introduction," to the whole idea, much as I continue to acknowledge that all ideas remain in flux. I intend to go on with my study of how we human beings grapple with uncertainty, to read what others have to say, and, above all to write down my observations from time to time. I paraphrase the immortal words of Mr. Toad in Kenneth Grahame's *Wind in the Willows:* "Believe me my young friend, there is nothing—absolutely nothing—half so much worth doing as simply messing about in *words.*"

I conclude *The Fantods of Risk* and begin my new travel with yet another haiku, my favorite form of poetry:

> Curiosity!
> I take a fork in the road
> With spring in my step.

Felix Kloman
November 2007

CHAPTER 1

Preliminary Conclusion: What *Is* Risk Management?

> Propose it, evince the evidence, consider the objections, reassert it in the conclusion. A narrative in itself—a little tired, perhaps, but it had served a thousand journalists before me.
>
> **Ian McEwan, *Enduring Love,* Random House, New York 1999**

I begin with a candid acknowledgement. I'm plagued by the fantods of risk (my state of restlessness) and I'm not really sure what risk management is or means. I don't know, but I remain infinitely curious! Perhaps curiosity, then, is the only method of curing the fantods

I first read the words "risk management" in late 1957, in my first job working for an insurance brokerage firm in Philadelphia, fresh from two years on the Pacific Ocean serving the United States Navy. I was intrigued by the term, as it seemed a broader and more challenging field than simply designing and selling commercial insurance. In the ensuing fifty years, my intrigue has grown even as my understanding remained elusive. Thus, this series of essays begins with my current working hypothesis about this fascinating discipline. It nevertheless is still my "preliminary conclusion," subject to change.

"Risk management" has morphed from its original use as a euphemism for insurance buying into a rainbow of different interpretations and usages. It is now found in public policy pronouncements, financial trading, advice on investments, safety and security, politics, and in almost every aspect of our daily lives. That we have actually made some modest progress in managing life's uncertain affairs is more the result of some intelligent use of the ideas behind the phrase than of the convoluted semantics and unnecessary complexities offered by so many organizations and observers.

So, on the fiftieth anniversary of my introduction to the idea of risk management, I think it appropriate to try and whittle away the excess lard that encumbers the idea and suggest a fresh and brief definition of what we are talking about.

First, all of us, individuals and organizations alike, necessarily live in a fog of uncertainty. Peter Bernstein described it as "the bewildering jumble of facts, rumors, discontinuities, vagueness, and black uncertainty that make up the real world around us" (*Capital Ideas Evolving,* John Wiley & Sons, Inc, New York, 2007). Nassim Taleb, in *The Black Swan* (Random House, New York 2007) describes a "world that is dominated by the extreme, the unknown, and the very improbable (improbable according to our direct knowledge)—and all the while we spend our time engaged in small talk, focusing on the known and the repeated." There is no way we can know for certain what the next moment, day, month or year will bring. Candid acknowledgement of the fact of uncertainty may be contrary to the desire of the human species but it is essential for our constant evolution. Throughout history we've found that subscribing to some artificial explanation for unexpected events delays our ability to collect information and experience so that we can, slowly over time, begin to understand why things have occurred in the past and how we can better prepare ourselves for the uncertain future. In the past four hundred years, for example, we learned how to collect information and manipulate it so that we can create "risk," a modest measure of future likelihood and consequences, to enable us to make better decisions. Whether qualitative or quantitative, these measures are becoming the bases of how we decide to move ahead. We are slowly parting from a past of superstition, myth, archaic dogma and irrationality. Fate and the intervention of so-called "divine" creatures are slipping into the past of the human species. Even so, we must resist the intoxication of new knowledge. Richard Feynman described our condition in an essay in *The Pleasures of Finding Things Out* (Perseus Books, Cambridge 1999): "People search for certainty. But there *is* no certainty. You only think you know . . . . And most of your actions are based on incomplete knowledge and you really don't know what it is all about, or what the purpose of the world is, or know a great deal about other things. It is possible live and not know." So any management of risk begins with a frank acknowledgement that we really don't know! Instead of trying to avoid surprise we should relish it.

Second, I suggest some new definitions. My goal is to make each as brief as possible, simply because they are easier to remember.

The word *risk* requires a definition, as it is the linchpin of the idea.

Risk is a measure of the probable likelihood, consequences and timing of an event.

A critical ingredient of risk is that an outcome may be *either favorable or unfavorable*, or, in some instances, a combination of both, perhaps depending on how we respond to the event. Risk is a "measure" of possibility; it is *not* an event, situation or physical structure.

It is also best described as a *range* of outcomes—likelihoods and consequences—often shown as a mathematical distribution based on prior data. But do not be deluded by these data! Outliers, extreme events, "unknown unknowns" often bring enormous consequences and remain beyond our capacity to measure.

How, then, do we define the idea of trying to manage risk?

Risk Management is a discipline for dealing with uncertainty.

It is a controlled and more logical, more rational means of understanding the past and projecting possible alternative futures so that we can make *better decisions.* It is a *discipline,* not a profession, as it, so far, lacks a common body of knowledge. It is still evolving and may always be evolving. Its proper focus is uncertainty and that includes the acknowledgement that nothing, absolutely nothing (to borrow the phrase from *Wind in the Willows*) is certain. Perhaps Heisenberg's principle goes well beyond physics!

Most definitions of risk management are too long and wrapped in business jargon. Here is recent example of a useless tautology (the perpetrator remains *incognito)*

> The purpose of risk management is to achieve project or business objectives through the systematic identification, assessment and management of risk.

A better one comes from the Casualty Actuarial Society in the United States:

> Enterprise risk management is the *discipline* by which an organization in any industry assesses, controls, exploits, finances and monitors risks from all sources for the purpose of increasing the organization's short- and long-term value to its shareholders.

The best current definition is that from the Australian Standards/New Zealand Standards 4360:2004:

> Risk management is the culture, processes and structures that are directed towards realizing potential opportunities whilst managing adverse effects.

The last two are better but still too wordy. Can you remember either of them? "A discipline for dealing with uncertainty" is brief and memorable.

Third, how do we apply risk management to individual and organizational decision-making? The conscious and subconscious uses of experience and information have been part of the genetic makeup of the human species since we first crawled out of the water. We accumulate knowledge from what we see and hear, from teachings, genetic heritage and shared experiences, creating from them rough heuristics, or rules-of-thumb, to use as guides. More recently we've developed the ideas of probability mathematics and decision theory to improve how we decide. Even as we rely more on numbers we must acknowledge that moral (and qualitative) factors are as important as economic. Add to that mixture the problem of the totally unexpected, the random nature of the outliers that we can't even imagine, and we find that this newly-developed "process" isn't the final answer.

If the process of managing risk to make better decisions is basically instinctual, how best to describe it for application in organizations? I suggest again a briefer approach.

The risk management process: Risk Analysis and Risk Response.

Risk analysis has three logical sub-steps:

Event identification: possible unexpected events, situations, contingencies, and/or sequences of events, whether favorable or unfavorable. Imagining the never-experienced outliers remains a real problem.

Risk assessment: qualitative and quantitative estimates of the ranges (distribution) of likelihood, consequences, timing and assessment credibility for events, using multiple perceptions of affected stakeholders. And always consider those nasty outliers!

Evaluation: consider probable and possible effects on an organization, its reputation, its economic capital, and, most importantly, its stakeholders.

Risk response also includes three sub-steps:

Control: mechanisms, incentives and penalties to improve the possibility of favorable and reduce the possibility of unfavorable outcomes.

Contingency planning: preparation for the predicted *plus* the most extreme of outcomes, the "tails" and "outliers" that too many disregard. Consequence always trumps likelihood! Preparedness is better than prediction.

Communications: creation of an on-going, two-way dialogue with *all* stakeholders on key elements of analyses and responses and on how well the organization is prepared for the unexpected.

This process leads to making one decision, and then another, and altering decisions, on a continuous basis.

Finally, what is the goal of risk management?

The goal of risk management is to build and maintain the confidence of stakeholders in the organization.

Trust, the most important asset of any organization, is, by definition, difficult to measure. It can change momentarily and be radically different from one group of stakeholders to another. Yet this is and must be the focus of an organization. Trust and confidence come first. Capital assets, earning power, skills of employees, management, credit lines, and quality of products or services are all secondary.

So, to restate these definitions, we begin by acknowledging that we exist in a perpetual fog of uncertainty. We can, with skill and luck, translate *some* of this fog into "risk," enabling us to make more informed decisions about the future. Our approach is to think about risk more intelligently and then do something about it.

That is risk management, or at least it is how I interpret it some fifty years after my first glimpse of the idea.

CHAPTER 2

Things That Go Bump in the Night

This chapter opens with a paper published by Zurich Insurance Company in its focus26, in 1999, and revised from a speech in London on Sept. 21, 1993 and a subsequent paper entitled "Considering Catastrophes" in Risk Management Reports, September/October 1993. It has been modified to reflect more recent developments. Two other comments follow, one on terrorism and the other on paleoclimatology.

Things That Go Bump in the Night

> "From ghoulies and ghosties and long-leggety beasties,
> And things that go bump in the night,
> Good Lord, deliver us."

This old Cornish prayer is a fervent plea to send elsewhere misfortune, disasters and catastrophes. But, as the media remind us each day, these "bumps in the night" are continuing parts of our lives. They are the black clouds gathering over our enjoyment of life. Why do they worry us so? Why are we so obsessed with these events?

First, what are "catastrophes?" Many are natural developments of weather or tectonic movement. We count Galveston (1900), Labor Day (1938), and then Andrew, Hugo, and Georges and Mitch (1998) and Katrina and Rita (2005) among the most horrendous hurricanes in North America. Major earthquakes include San Francisco, China, and, more recently, Loma Prieta, Longridge, Kobe and Pakistan. Volcanic eruptions include Krakatoa and, of course, the Indonesia tsunami of 2004. The 1997 Red River floods and the 1998 New England/Canadian ice storm are other examples. Environmental and technological disasters include Bhopal, Seveso, Chernobyl, Exxon Valdez, Challenger/Columbia, and Piper Alpha. Wars and their related human upheavals generally top the lists, counting the Civil War in the United States, World Wars I and II, genocides in Armenia, the Soviet Union, Germany, Cambodia, and China, and the more recent events in Bosnia, Kosovo, Kenya, Tanzania, Rwanda, Burundi, Congo, Sudan, Iraq, and Afghanistan. Add also periodic pandemics (see influenza 1918-1920). These are calamities, distortions to life's equanimity, challenges to our conceit in ever-continuing progress, shocks to our systems, enhanced of late by the increasing power of media to tell us of them instantly and in gory detail. The definition of a "catastrophe" used by the Swiss Reinsurance Company thus seems a bit callous in light of the enormous emotional trauma, but it is a useful starting point for calculation: *over 100 deaths and over US$100 million in losses*. The human species has always had a morbid fascination with the unexpectedly awful but this fascination seems to have escalated of late. No longer do we, like Captain MacWhirr of the *Nan Shan*, understate a typhoon as "a bit of dirty weather." We now embellish and adorn each catastrophe, distorting our perspectives in relation to other daily misfortunes.

My focus in this paper is on natural disasters. Our goal is, first, to try and forecast these events; second, to reduce loss of life, injury and damage; and third, to ameliorate the global emotional and financial effects as far as possible. Response and recovery alone aren't enough. Many now believe that our technological, communication, and economic powers enable us to mitigate catastrophes before they occur. This is the thesis of contingency planning. But is this possible?

I have three observations and three suggestions.

Three Observations

First, catastrophes are inevitable. Second, our current methods of financing catastrophe losses may actually *increase* their probable consequences. Third, while the sophistication of global catastrophe communications can build risk awareness and early warning, they can, at the same time, exacerbate effects.

The inescapable nature of catastrophe. Disasters belong to human history. Our growing knowledge and skills (dams, levees, understanding plate tectonics, weather forecasting) are formidable, yet they seem incapable of eliminating their effects. In Bangladesh, the Ganges regularly floods the delta, killing and injuring thousands. Hurricanes or typhoons savage the Caribbean/Atlantic and the South China Sea annually. William McNeill, writing in *Daedalus* some years ago, suggested that, despite gains in technology and understanding nature, we may be subject to a "law of conservation of catastrophe" that says the more we learn and do, the more we create conditions leading to the next one. The solutions to one crisis pave the way for some equal or greater future disaster." Witness the rush to rebuild in flood, earthquake and windstorm-prone areas, be it along the Atlantic, the Mississippi, or the Ganges. McNeill's Law suggests we are predestined for disaster.

The Red Cross reports a "significant natural disaster" each week somewhere in the world. Reinsurers Swiss Re and Munich Re report a rise in both the frequency and the economic severity of insured disaster events over the past two decades. Global warming and El Niño are undoubtedly factors, but the biggest contributors are the sheer growth in the number of people on this globe, their concentration, particularly in disaster-prone areas, and the escalation of economic values. Weather experts suggest, in the past 200 years, we have lived through a relatively benign period for natural upheavals, and that the earth is now entering a new period of greater volatility. Population growth, forecast to increase to 9.2 billion by 2050, most of it in the under-developed world, alone makes the McNeill "Law" believable. Under these conditions, a Hugo of $4 billion becomes an Andrew of $18 billion, which in turn will be the yet nameless windstorm of 2010 with an economic loss of $100 billion! The1991 Bangladesh cyclone and flood that killed 140,000, left three million homeless and cost $2.4 billion, could, in less than two decades, be *one hundred* times as devastating.

Financing catastrophes The costs of most world catastrophes are covered by local and governmental funding, with support from international relief agencies. In more economically advanced nations, commercial insurance plays a larger role, but the lion's share (probably over 90%) still falls on governments and public and private public agencies, such as FEMA (Federal Emergency Management Agency) in the United States. In the Kobe earthquake, some 85% of the loss was borne by government. Despite its relatively nominal role in catastrophe financing, the non-life insurance industry remains apprehensive of the effect of a major disaster on its finances. Some of the causes of this apprehension are of its own making: inadequate underwriting for almost a half-century, its inability, in many countries, to set aside long-term catastrophe reserves on a tax-efficient basis, and the questionable nature of its reserves. More than a decade ago, in 1993, the industry financial analyst Myron Picoult, in New York, warned, "In all the years we have covered the property/casualty industry, we have never seen it in worse financial shape." In 1998, he was no more sanguine: "The pit may be deeper . . . because of . . . the erosion of balance sheet strengths by many insurers that are compromising the integrity of their balance sheets to buttress near-term earnings." Is the industry in any better shape today? Picoult remains skeptical: "the cloud of mediocrity is growing," he said in early 2007, as the non-life industry fails to take advantage of new technology, scorns innovation, and submits to less than stellar leadership.

Michael Lewis, writing in *The New York Times Magazine* on August 26. 2007 ("In Nature's Casino") warned that the catastrophe exposure for non-life insurance companies is in excess of $500 billion, while these insurers have less that 10% of that amount in payment capacity.

Since governmental financing of disasters is driven by short-term political considerations, those at risk are seldom required to take even limited preventive steps and, post-loss, they may be allowed to rebuild at the same site with only modest changes. Good examples are the recent experiences in New Orleans and along the Gulf Coast. Governments are disinclined to enforce building codes (after all, these people are *voters!)*, and the private sector, including banks and insurers, compliantly follow, fearing regulatory reprisal. Despite this, some observers argue the private insurance industry can be a key catalyst introducing a combination of risk reduction measures and financially secure reimbursements for a portion of losses. This is the thesis of *Paying the Price,* a 1998 study of the role of insurance against natural disasters in the United States, written and edited by Howard Kunreuther and Richard J. Roth, Sr.

The role of the media For three weeks in the autumn of 1998, IDNDR (International Decade for Natural Disaster Reduction), a Geneva-based United Nations project team, used the Internet to conduct a symposium on the role of the media in natural disasters. One participant suggested that the media might "itself be the disaster," because of its proclivity to sensationalism. He noted that the media may take less interest in the warnings than in the actual events, and that it is apt to "create its own facts" in the absence of experts. The symposium concluded that the media must become full partners in disaster planning as well as reporting, to educate the audience worldwide about prevention and recovery. Their role is critical to "empowering individuals to learn, understand and act." Obviously an irresponsible and uninformed media adds to confusion, loss of life, injury and economic damages. The IDNDR group concluded, "Local, regional and national authorities must understand media needs and create partnerships to provide a structured and coordinated means of distributing information in a format and style that guarantees its widest possible exposure." Add to this list of cooperating organizations the representatives of the private sector: financial institutions, insurers, and relief agencies. This United Nations effort continues with the ISDR, International Strategy for Disaster Reduction.

The media may also lull people into a false sense of security. In 1997, during the Red River of the North floods in North Dakota and Minnesota, the press, radio and television repeated scientific predictions of a 49-foot crest, within existing levees, failing to note the possibility of a higher crest. This led to under-preparation and the eventual displacement of 50,000 people.

Three Suggestions

First, we must accept more individual responsibility. Second, like the Biblical admonition to set aside something in the full years for the fallow ones, we need a new and different tax approach to catastrophe reserves. Third, public and private cooperation is essential.

Individual responsibility When individuals and organizations deliberately expose people or property to a known potential catastrophe, failing to use state-of-the-art preventive steps, they must pay a price. Too often public and private financing is excessively generous. Too often politicians and regulators labor under the illusion that owners have an absolute "right" to use their property in any fashion and a corollary "right" to buy cheap insurance or to recover from government funds when the inevitable occurs. Too often we simply absolve people of their responsibilities for prudence.

This must change. We must become rigorous in risk assessment. The insurance industry has begun this effort, building and using new predictive models to expand our knowledge of the likelihood disasters and their consequences. We must adopt and enforce new building codes, security standards and emergency planning protocols, all with tangible support from lenders, shareholders, the building trades, and government. Governmental funding should be *excess* of any commercial insurance that was or *could have been* purchased. Insurance should require higher levels of individual and corporate participation. Finally, as responsible individuals, we must reserve our inherent skepticism of scientific forecasts, recognizing that the impossible can occur.

Better reserving Current accounting rules and tax regulations in North America and elsewhere in much of the world actively inhibit the creation of catastrophe reserves. Organizations and insurers must argue for some form of tax-efficient catastrophe reserving, also known as equalization reserves. They should be permitted to corporations and insurers alike. The growing use of catastrophe bonds, using the capital markets, is an opportunity to create reserve funds where none now exist, but cat bonds remain experimental since they require a large, liquid, and consistent base of long-term investors. Organizations, governments and investors will never solve responsible catastrophe financing if all three remain consumed with short-term thinking. We need a long-term view to respond intelligently to the financial implications of catastrophes.

Public and private cooperation Although their effects are primarily local, catastrophes are global problems. They send ripples throughout the world economy. We must accept some degree of global responsibility for them. Dumping their financial results in a limited arena can mean the bankruptcies of smaller governments and insurers and even regional economies. The response begins, first, with renewed individual responsibility, noted above. The private sector, including relief agencies and the insurance industry, follows. Above them, national governments and regional consort a step in. In 1992, the United Nations suggested this form of coordinated response through a proposed UN Disaster Relief Office, or UNDRO. It targeted reductions of 50% for loss of life and 10% to 40% in financial losses. It is a dual "preparedness" plus "emergency response" approach to crisis management. It requires close collaboration among the various private sector groups (insurers, nonprofit relief agencies, banks, investment markets, real estate organizations) and public sector representatives (local, state, provincial, and national governments, regional consortia, international groups). An UNDRO will require funding comparable to the International Monetary Fund, perhaps $100 to $250 billion, plus additional commitments in the event of a sequence of disasters.

Are these proposals practical? The optimist sees their inherent rationality. The pessimist acknowledges their political and economic limitations. Can we wait for catastrophes to savage a financial institution like the insurance industry before we construct a workable system? I hope not. Faced with the inevitability of catastrophic events and the human and economic misery they create, and with the inability of the conventional non-life insurance market to play a material role in financing them, we must consider rebuilding personal and organizational accountability, rationalizing reserving mechanisms, and creating greater public and private collaboration.

The potential for disaster shouldn't petrify us into a rigid risk-aversion mentality. Instead, as the poet and novelist Patrick O'Brian reminds us:

> Every calamity, by thought refined,
> Inspirits and adorns the thinking mind.

Catastrophes are not always natural. September 11, 2001 reminded us of that. So too did July 7, 2005, the date of the London Underground (subway) and bus bombings.

London—July 7, 2005

On the evening of July 6, I started reading *Saturday,* Ian McEwan's novel of a neurosurgeon's life in London, a deeply introspective reflection on one day's events. It begins with the sighting of a burning airplane, "some hours before dawn," that leads him to imagine a possible terrorist attack on the city. I dropped off to sleep after the first chapter and awoke to find not a simple accident and no fatalities, as in the book, but the appalling carnage of four suicide bombers, the dead and wounded in the Underground and on the bus, and the continuation of raw terror.

Is there any significance to this unusual connection of mine or to the prescient words of McEwan? That this event was anticipated goes without question. Premonition or not, the simple statistics of the post-9/11 world and the calculations of the quants warned us to expect another New York, Bali, Madrid. We can't avoid the daily headlines from Iraq and Afghanistan. July 7 is stark reminder of the gulf that exists in our world today. On one side is a modern, individualistic, mostly secular group that is, above all, comfortable with uncertainty—in economics, politics, science and philosophy. On the other side, living almost 800 years in the past, is a group that despises the outward trappings of a modern world, caught in regressive ideologies based on the immoveable readings of an ancient text by self-appointed priests, imams, mullahs and ayatollahs. This is hardly a new story: throughout history, as McEwan notes in his novel, "the pursuit of utopia ends up licensing every form of excess, all ruthless means of its realization." While the current terror is primarily attributable to radical Islamists, their vision is similar to those who preceded them (and inevitably, to others who follow). Again, McEwan: "Out in the real world there exist detailed plans, visionary projects for peaceable realms, all conflicts resolved, happiness for everyone, for ever—mirages for which people are prepared to die and kill. Christ's kingdom on earth, the workers' paradise, the ideal Islamic state." These illusions are seductive and, when set in the minds of fanatics, become bloodthirsty.

So our great challenge for the next fifty-plus years must be to convince those trapped in their "certainty" of the past to adopt more tolerant view. This challenge is as important in what we refer to as the "West" as it is in the Middle East and Asia. It directly affects those of us who practice the discipline of risk management because our discipline teaches us to accept and even revel in uncertainty.

My sympathy goes out to all Londoners, who have already demonstrated the same resilience they showed under the onslaught of the Luftwaffe, V-1 buzz bombs and V-2 rockets in the Second World War. Londoners have responded just as New Yorkers and the citizens of Madrid. The constant threat of a senseless terrorist act will be the central risk management issue for many years to come. Other cities will suffer similar acts, just as Bali, Belfast, Tokyo and Oklahoma City have experienced them. Ian McEwan said the same halfway through his novel: "there will be more deaths on a similar scale (*referring to 9/11*), probably in this city (*London*)." Somehow we will learn how to meet and respond to this tidal wave of irrational fanaticism and to engage all those trapped in their inability to accept uncertainty. But can we do so without sacrificing in the process our own standards and liberties?

At the very end of the book McEwan comments: "London, his small part of it, lies wide open, impossible to defend, waiting for the bomb, like hundreds of other cities. Rush hour will be a convenient time." McEwan knew it; the terrorists knew it; and we know it.

Terrorism is not easily susceptible to the models of quantitative analysis. It requires a sense of history, patience and a willingness to embark on a slow and tedious track of persuasion. At the same time we must maintain the openness and tolerance of our societies. Yes, it is a "war," but it must employ not just warriors and arms but minds and ideas.

> . . . there must have been survival advantage in dreaming up bad outcomes and scheming to avoid them. This trick of dark imagining is one legacy of natural selection in a dangerous world.
>
> . . . misery is more amenable to analysis.
>
> **Ian McEwan, *Saturday,* Doubleday, New York 2005**

Paleoclimatology is beginning to tell us more about this earth on which we live and its propensity for periodic disruption.

"The earth is a twitchy system."

What do the Middle Eastern empire of Akkad, the Mayan civilization of Central America, the Old Kingdom of Egypt and the Tiwanaku civilization in the Andes have in common with our world today? The first four collapsed as the result of abrupt and extreme climate changes, earth "twitches," the same types of change that could occur within the next 50 years. While global warming has been a major topic of concern for many years, Elizabeth Kolbert, in a series of three articles in *The New Yorker* (April 25, May 2 and May 9, 2005), brings a fresh and disturbing view, based on recent discoveries of paleoclimatology.

She reports new evidence of the potential for "sudden and unpredictable reversals" in climate. It isn't just that, over the past 150 years, industrialized society on this earth has been pumping carbon dioxide into our atmosphere to the point where it is reaching a level unprecedented in the last 100,000 years, the time that *homo sapiens* has developed and spread around the globe as the dominant species. New discoveries, especially from cores drilled into the Greenland ice cap, show that rapid and disruptive climate changes have been far more frequent than we realized. Our "civilization," dating back about 10,000 years, has been the beneficiary of a relatively benign climate, fostering the spread of humans around the globe. Kolbert writes, "Since our species evolved, average temperatures have never been more than two or three degrees higher than they are right now. The planet is now nearly as warm as it has been at any point in the last four hundred and twenty thousand years!" But ice cores and other data (see also her article "Ice Memory," *The New Yorker,* January 7, 2002) provide "overwhelming empirical evidence" of "abrupt climate changes." Many scientists now believe that we may be approaching the end of this "benign" period, known as the Eocene, and that we should be preparing for rapid and wrenching changes.

The literature of global warming already suggests changes such as rising sea levels, loss of snow cover, altered patterns of vegetation and agriculture, warmer temperatures and directional variations in critical ocean currents, such as the Gulf Stream that warms Northern Europe. As prior large and sophisticated cultures "have already been undone by climate change," is it possible that ours will follow a similar path? Her prognosis, supporting by many scientists whom she interviewed for this series, is not good. Robert de Menocil, at the Lamont-Doherty Earth Sciences Laboratory of Columbia University is gloomy: "The thing they couldn't prepare for was the same thing we won't prepare for, because in their case they didn't know about it and in our case the political system can't listen to it. And that is the climate system has much greater things in store for us than we think." Here is Marty Hoffert at New York University: "I'm not sure we can solve the problem. I hope we can. I think we have a shot. I mean, it may be that we're not going to solve global warming (and) the earth is going to become an ecological disaster." To Kolbert, global warming has the potential of becoming "the tragedy of the commons, writ large."

Does everyone agree on the potential for this disaster? While Kolbert writes, "in legitimate scientific circles, it is virtually impossible to find evidence of disagreement over the fundamentals of global warming," there are dissenters. I've already written about Bjorn Lomborg and his 2001 book, *The Skeptical Environmentalist,* (Columbia University Press), a balanced contrary view that any risk manager should read. Add to his views those of Richard Lindzen at MIT. Lindzen agrees about the evidence on the current warming trend and the increase in the amount of carbon dioxide that human activities have pumped into our atmosphere. What he questions is the net effect of this on our climate. Kolbert suggests that the preponderance of evidence argues in favor of more dramatic action, now. She reports on the practical suggestions of Robert Socolow, an engineering professor at Princeton. Rather than try and tackle the entire gamut of carbon dioxide pollution, he proposes a series of separate "wedges," each of which has greater political potential for adoption in the next few years. Some of these, for example, include rapid development of alternative energy sources, such as photovoltaic cells, wind electricity, and new nuclear facilities, a tax on carbon, and modification of automobiles (use them half as much; make them twice as energy efficient).

Kolbert concludes that the major problem is “political apathy” on a global basis. A letter writer in the succeeding issue of *The New Yorker* (June 13-20) also warned that we are “incapable of thinking in time frames exceeding our own life spans.”

This series is a warning to all risk managers. It also calls to mind a quote I read four years ago from the singer and environmentalist Pete Seeger: “I’ve come to the conclusion that there is nothing good that doesn’t have bad consequences and nothing bad that doesn’t have good consequences.” (Quoted by Matthew Purdy in The *New York Times,* July 22, 2001).

I hope Seeger is right.

CHAPTER 3

Katrina and What It Can Tell Us

The hurricane Katrina, *an August/September 2005 disaster, was an international event, not so much for its direct human and economic consequences as for its demonstration of inadequate planning, incompetent emergency response, and illogical follow-up.* Katrina *prompted several comments from me in* Risk Management Reports.

> The risks of global catastrophe are greater and more numerous than is commonly supposed, and they are growing, probably rapidly.
>
> **Richard A. Posner, *Catastrophe: Risk and Response,***
> **Oxford University Press, Oxford 2004**

Katrina and Evacuation

When I started writing the following words on August 15, 2005, *Katrina* wasn't close to my radar screen. Several articles on evacuation had piqued my interest, so I let my thoughts run and finished the article. Now, two days following the disastrous effects of the hurricane that savaged the south Florida, Louisiana, and Mississippi shores, I am rewriting my comments in light of the enormous cost in lives, injuries and economic disruption caused by *Katrina.*

* * *

One of the most difficult military evolutions is retreat, moving troops from a position of danger to safety at minimum cost. Three examples come to mind: George Washington's night escape from Brooklyn to Manhattan Island in 1776 without the loss of a single soldier, the British Army's remarkable 1940 evacuation from Dunkirk in the Second World War, and the incredible exploit of Sir Ernest Shackleton bringing back to the Falkland Islands the entire *Endurance* crew of his Antarctic expedition (1914-1916), also without loss of life. These examples build an appreciation of both the importance of planned evacuation and the difficulty of success.

What we require, every time, is early consideration of possible unexpected events that could force reaction, and pre-planning for *all* contingencies. Even with those ingredients in place, leadership, imagination and luck remain necessary.

In today's crowded cities and suburbs, the threats of terrorism and natural disaster are even more serious, requiring governments to create and test meticulous plans for rapid movements of tens to hundreds of thousands of people in a short period of time. Organization risk managers face the same requirements, especially when responsible for many employees in a single location or region.

Transportation is the first essential ingredient in emergency planning and evacuation. Two challenging articles address this subject in the August 2005 issue of *Natural Hazards Review,* the quarterly publication of the Natural Hazards Research and Applications Information Center of the University of Colorado and the American Society of Civil Engineers. Given the results of *Katrina,* their timing could not be better. Three members of the faculty of Louisiana State University plus a Texas engineer review state evacuation practices for the rapid movement of large populations. They use as an example moving the residents of New Orleans to higher ground in the face of windstorm and flood, something that the government attempted just before *Katrina.* It is not only planning, preparation and response, but, perhaps more important, the communication with the general populace and the detailed control of traffic that stand between success and a disaster accentuated by panic. The authors describe a relatively new development, the "planned use of contra-flow freeway operations" as a technique to move a large segment of the population quickly to safe ground. In a pending disaster, entering an "off" ramp may be the key to survival. Another critical area is distributing "timely, accurate, and useful information to evacuees." Any organizational risk manager should be familiar with the developing integration of weather and traffic systems.

Given the breeches of several levees following *Katrina* and the subsequent flooding of 80% of the city, New Orleans was largely uninhabitable for many weeks. This poses another problem: how to manage the evacuees, not only the original 80% that escaped before the storm but also the remaining 20% later ordered away. Relocation, return and reconstruction require enormous resources and considerable time, but, just as the world responded to the December 2004 Indonesian tsunami, it is evident that a resurgent New Orleans and Biloxi will appear in due course. Over the longer term, however, we will begin to wonder about the rationality of continuing to site critical oil and natural gas refining capacity in that area as well as a major city, most of which is eight to ten feet under the level of the sea and the river.

This entire subject of emergency and continuity planning will be the subject of three simultaneous conferences on November 16-17, 2005, in London, Munich and Mumbai. They are all offshoots of this past January's World Conference on Disaster Recovery, in Kobe, which serendipitously followed immediately after the Indonesian tsunami. Coming now just after *Katrina,* they will focus attention on the practical opportunities for the private and public sectors to cooperate in disaster reduction and recovery. Much of this, of course, depends on a solid collaboration among governments (local, provincial and national) and the many facets of the private sector. *Katrina* will provide examples of successes and failures. This is an area where organizational risk managers can and should take leadership initiative. Pre-disaster risk assessments, immediate disaster response and post-disaster recovery and resilience require an understanding not only of your own immediate situation, but also of what others are doing (or not doing).

Retreat and evacuation are critical tactics for a long-range strategy of success. Retreat is never a goodbye but rather a prelude to a new hello, as both George Washington and Winston Churchill proved.

Time encourages reflection, and I returned to the implications of Katrina *some months later.*

Katrina Again

The disaster in Louisiana and Mississippi prompts not only compassion for all those affected by *Katrina* but also incomprehension about how we could have permitted such loss of life, injuries and economic damage in light or prior warnings. It is a classic lesson for those who practice some form of risk management. It is not enough to make sophisticated projections of the results of a direct hit or near miss of a major extreme event. Assessments and warnings are useless unless they persuade "people," meaning both leaders and followers in the public and private sector, to take effective action. Risk assessment is not enough; risk response is the critical element of our process.

Despite numerous warnings about the potential for disaster in Louisiana (I have in my own files detailed assessments from the 1960s and 1970s), little or nothing was done. The residents of the Gulf Coast in effect said, "Come ahead and kiss me, Kate," as they awaited the inevitable. The emergency planning was equally unconscionable, given what leaders knew. After *Katrina*, *The New Yorker* reprinted a piece by John McPhee, first published in *1987* (!), citing why New Orleans and the Mississippi were disasters waiting to happen. They remain future disasters today, even after *Katrina*! That original article is stuffed in my files. I also found another one, this time from the November 2004 issue of *Natural Hazards Observer,* asking "What if Hurricane *Ivan* Had Not Missed New Orleans?" *Ivan*, in 2004, veered instead to hit Alabama, but the author of this piece, Shirley Laska, from the University of New Orleans, predicted in an uncanny way almost every detail of the carnage left by *Katrina*. She correctly saw that a large portion of the city's inhabitants would require immediate help to evacuate: "For those without means, the medically-challenged residents without personal transportation, and the homeless, evacuation requires significant assistance." Her prediction of estimated costs "exceeding $100 billion" was sadly correct: the first estimate published in *The New York Times* on

September 3, 2005, put the "economic toll at $100 billion." Mark Fischetti, also writing in the *Times,* on September 2, had it right: "Thus, in true American fashion, we ignored an inevitable problem until disaster focused our attention." It isn't that these earlier warnings were not credible. They were, but they were not heeded. Federal funds meant to shore up levees were diverted. Numerous reports from local academia and working committees were filed away. Those who were risk alert knew what could happen, but they were unable to translate their knowledge into meaningful pre-event responses.

Even with all the attention focused on the recovery from *Katrina*, including the re-flooding caused by *Rita*, few will acknowledge that re-building New Orleans, with a smaller population, with habitation only on higher ground, and with substantial improvement to the levees, *still* exposes this entire region to a similar disaster, either from the south (a Category 4 or 5 hurricane) or from the north (the Mississippi overflows and floods the city, or perhaps worse, it alters its course along the Atchafalaya, something that will happen inevitably, leaving New Orleans without a port). *Simply put, this city is untenable, despite its rich history and culture.* Is the American public willing to pay through the nose to rebuild a second time?

I find it hard to believe that, as a region and as a nation, we have disregarded all these warnings over more than a half-century. Our disregard is magnified by the inanity of some of the proposed responses. To throw billions in Federal and relief money at the problem won't solve the underlying difficulty, even though it is the easy political way out. We should be wiser than this!

As for economic repercussions, I already hear of plaintiffs' attorneys who propose suits to force insurance companies to pay more than they intended or for which they are legally obligated. Most conventional insurance provides coverage for wind and wind-driven water damage, with losses attributable to "flood" covered under federal-government-subsidized policies. Yes, insurers are complicit to some degree for selling polices with an implication of full coverage, but is that a reason to sandbag them? The basic problem is that only a small percentage of home and business owners carried any flood insurance at all, despite its availability. One state is suing insurers to force them to pay for *all* losses, including those caused by flood, arguing that to do otherwise would be "unconscionable." If the well-understood and common forms of insurance contracts are to be broken after every disaster, we risk undermining the entire insurance industry. I've been critical of the inefficiencies and ineptitude of this industry for some time, but I cannot support in any way, shape or form dismantling it by class action suits and ill-advised state attorneys general. The result would lead to government having to respond to all claims in the future. *The Economist* had the right idea when it wrote, on September 17, 2005: "The cleanest approach would be to get rid of federal insurance entirely and let the private market price the risks of living below sea level or in flood-prone areas (*and, I would add, in areas subject to extreme winds and earthquakes).*" It went on: "The problem is that the inevitability of government bail-outs will persuade many not to pay up. An alternative would be to make natural disaster insurance (covering floods, earthquakes, avalanches and so on) obligatory, with premiums more closely reflecting the risk." Until and unless we place more of the financial burden on those who elect to put themselves in harm's way, and turn away when they call for help after their barns have burned, we will follow this financial spiral to the bottom. And if we cannot find a reasonable solution in short order, we risk losing private sector risk financing.

These gloomy thoughts recalled three books I read during the summer of 2005, all concerned with "catastrophe." What does this word mean to us? We have numerical scales for measuring various extreme events, such as the arithmetic Saffir-Simpson scale for hurricanes (Category 5 being the worst: winds over 135 knots) and Beaufort scale for wind speeds. We use the logarithmic Modified Mercalli scale for measuring the intensity (and damage potential) of earthquakes. On the other hand we use a basket of almost interchangeable words to describe extreme events, words that ought be refined. A "crisis" could be the first step in such a scale, perhaps defined as an unstable condition requiring immediate response. A second level might be "disaster," an "occurrence causing widespread destruction and distress," according to my dictionary. While "catastrophe" is listed as a synonym for "disaster," I sense that it describes more than that, a broader calamity, one along the lines of the 2004 tsunami and the 2005 *Katrina*. But how do we describe an even broader destructive and calamitous event? Is "Armageddon" the right term, a word that connotes a sense of finality for the human race?

Two of the best books of 2005 address this idea of Armageddon. The first is Jared Diamond's *Collapse: How Societies Choose to Fail or Succeed* (Viking, New York 2005). It is a paean to paleobotony, the science of discovering the past through determining what plants lived and died and what humans ate, and through using newly-available scientific tools. Paleobotony now opens up a fresh view of many prior civilizations, including several that ceased to exist for reasons we have been unable to determine before this time. Diamond, whose earlier *Guns, Germs and Steel* won a Pulitzer Prize, tells the stories of several current societies in which environmental changes are taking place, including the State of Montana, Rwanda, Haiti, Dominican Republic, China and Australia, and compares them to others from the past, such as Easter, Pitcairn and Henderson islands in the Pacific, the Anasazi civilization in New Mexico, the Mayans, and the settlements in Iceland and Greenland. Some of these past civilizations collapsed and some survived. Those that collapsed inevitably showed a combination of human hubris and inexorable environmental changes, some natural and some man-made.

Diamond's book has four basic themes:

1. "The interactions of human environmental impact and climate change."
2. "Environmental and population problems spilling over into warfare."
3. "The danger of complex non-self-sufficient societies dependent on imports and exports."
4. "Societies collapsing swiftly after attaining peak population numbers and power."

The survival of Scandinavians in Iceland stands in contrast to their disappearance in Greenland, a tale of adaptation in the first case and the victory of rigid ideology over common sense in the second. But Diamond's most telling example is the case of the extinction of a once flourishing civilization on Easter Island, where a combination of population growth and man-made destruction of the natural environment led to its inevitable decline. "What really counts is not the number of people alone, but their impact on the environment." The illustration of Easter Island should give us pause, as not only is the earth's total population growing (from 6 billion today to a forecast 9.2 billion by 2050), but also the number of people with a dramatically higher effect on the environment is growing even faster, as developing nations discover and copy the rapacious appetites of their developed counterparts.

Diamond argues "Life is full of agonizing choices based on trade-offs, but that's the cruelest trade-off that we shall have to resolve: encouraging and helping all people to achieve a higher standard of living without thereby undermining that standard through overstressing global resources." He concludes on a cautious and optimistic note, suggesting that most of our problems are soluble, that more people in this world are now aware of and interested in environmental problems, that there is a growing willingness to make painful decisions about "old values," and that the global flow of information allows us to learn from the mistakes of others. *Collapse* is a perfect primer for risk management.

The second book is a literary discussion, almost a Socratic conversation with the author, on the entire risk management method, applied to "catastrophic risks." Written by Richard Posner, a judge on the US Appeals Court in Chicago, *Catastrophe: Risk and Response,* (Oxford University Press 2004) is an interdisciplinary approach to risk analyses and responses for four categories of extreme events of Doomsday proportions. They are the very events that, because their relative unlikelihood and horrendous consequences, we avoid thinking about.

Posner defines catastrophes as events that "threaten the survival of the human race," ones with very low near-term probabilities and enormous consequences (these are *Armageddons* on my scale). They come in four categories:

1. *Natural disaster* His principal example is a large asteroid of a diameter of a mile or greater hitting the earth, similar to the one that helped destroy the dinosaurs. One quarter of the human population would be dead in 24 hours and the rest would follow in short order.
2. *Laboratory or scientific accident* One of the new particle accelerators inadvertently creates a new negatively-charged particle, called a strangelet, that, in a matter of seconds, compresses the earth to a "hyperdense sphere of less than 100 meters in diameter. Talk about "dark" matter! At least this extermination would be painless.
3. *Unintended yet man-made disaster* The gradual warming of the earth accelerates into a runaway greenhouse spiral that, in turn, creates a possible counter-reaction of global cloud cover, then global cooling, leading to a "snowball earth" or nuclear winter. I first read about this twist in several of Loren Eisley's books in the late 1960s.

4. *Deliberately perpetrated disaster* The accidental or deliberate use of nuclear devices or biological bombs by terrorists or a global pandemic kills millions.

The author's willingness to think the unthinkable mirrors a similar treatise by Herman Kahn, written at the height of the Cold War, *On Thermonuclear War,* in which he explored the results of such an engagement. As Posner writes, "The fact that something is unlikely to happen is no reason to ignore the risk of its happening, especially when the 'it' may be the extinction of the human race." Some may argue that we cannot possibly measure the potential for some of these Armageddon-like events. Posner counters: "To assume that risks can be ignored if they cannot be measured is a head-in-the-sand approach."

Take global warming and bio-terrorism as examples. "Conservatives seize on the existence of doubt about the magnitude or causality of global warming to oppose emission controls, while liberals seize on doubt concerning the likelihood of bio-terrorism to oppose limitations on granting visas to foreigners to do research on lethal pathogens. In neither case is the existence of doubt a valid ground for rejecting expert opinion. Doubt properly is an input into analysis rather than a substitute for analysis."

Posner leaves me with the sobering conclusion that the human species will, at some point, become extinct—"extinction is at the heart of creative destruction," he writes—and it is only a matter of when and by whose hand, our own or some "natural" event such as an asteroid.

The author suggests we adopt a more "interdisciplinary approach" to risk analysis and response, and he dissects many of the weaknesses in the analytical tools we now use. For example, relying on past data (the actuarial approach) is misleading: "When conditions are changing rapidly, predictions based on simple extrapolations from past experience are likely to be completely unreliable." Cost-benefit analyses are similarly flawed: we need to rethink their utility and methodology, but not dispense with them. Above all, we need to expand the "role of the social sciences, especially economics, statistics, cognitive psychology and the law" in the practice of risk management, plus expanding the scientific knowledge of lawyers. "Risk assessment is a seriously incomplete guide to decision making. Among the things it leaves out are the social benefits of dangerous technologies."

Posner's "conversation" suggests a series of possible steps to reduce the risks of catastrophic losses:

1. Build a more scientifically literate legal profession. As he says, "The scientific ignorance not of the public at large but of the people who count in making and implementing policy is perhaps remediable." I find this argument especially compelling in a day when prophets swamp us with such half-baked pseudo-scientific ideas as "creationism" and "intelligent design."
2. Consider special courts, national and international, whose judges are versed in science.

3. Create a Center for Catastrophe Risk Assessment and Response (The National Aeronautical and Space Agency—NASA—in the United States has been working since 1998 to discover, track and catalogue by 2008 90% of the potentially earth-threatening space objects greater than one kilometer in width, and, by 2020 90% of smaller objects, of 460 feet for more in width. It has made some progress but it has funding problems. Posner's thesis is that this effort should be multi-national, not just the work of one country.)
4. Consider new fiscal tools for reducing adverse results, such as taxes, tradable emission limits, subsidies for research and development on reducing carbon dioxide, etc.
5. Create an International Environmental Protection Agency and/or an International Bio-weaponry Agency.
6. Mandate a "catastrophe" risk review for all new science and technology projects.
7. Limit the study of critical science in the United States and Europe by foreigners.
8. Consider new and more stringent police methods.

While I have serious reservations about his last two suggestions, overall his prescriptions command attention.

Posner's willingness to consider both the "unthinkable" results of some current trends and technologies and also possible "unthinkable" responses is an example of the risk management approach at its best. His logic, clarity of phrase, and challenge to conventional ideas make this one of the best books I've read on our discipline.

Disasters, catastrophes or Armageddons, whatever we call them, require the development of new ways of analysis and comprehension. I find even more recent literature available. One source is *Catastrophe Risk Management,* a London-based periodical whose Spring 2005 issue included a set of well-written and perceptive articles gathered by its editor, Lee Coppack. She wrote, "Geographically-extenuated dependencies create new business continuity issues and multiple events exacerbate the demand surge that normally follows a catastrophic event." In 2005, political turmoil in Venezuela, the continuing and increasing civil war in Iraq, and *Katrina/Rita* combined to affect world oil prices and businesses everywhere. Just because the tsunami, hurricane or earthquake did not hit your property doesn't mean that you are free from their effects.

In that same issue James Arnell summarized many of the new modeling techniques used for catastrophes, most of which are also found in a book edited by Patricia Grossi and Howard Kunreuther, *Catastrophe Modeling: A New Approach to Managing Risk* (Springer, New York 2005). This is a set of thoughtful and practical essays on the use of models to assess portfolio risk, to deal with uncertainty, to communicate with selected stakeholder groups, and to develop risk management strategies for natural disasters and terrorism (an unnatural disaster). The editors enlisted support from three pre-eminent modeling groups, AIR Worldwide, EQE and Risk Management Solutions, whose models are now used by many insurers and reinsurers around the world.

Modeling is but one step toward understanding these extreme event risks by financially affected institutions. Another major remaining problem is how to reduce the propensity of individuals and businesses to locate themselves in areas prone to disasters, under the impression that someone will always bail them out. Outright prohibition seldom works and opening a federal bankroll after each event simply perpetuates the problem. A combination of regulatory coercion and economic persuasion is probably one solution but it has yet to be articulated intelligently and applied in specific situations. I can think of the flood-prone areas of Bangladesh and the coastal areas of the east and Gulf coasts of the United States. Land use planning is one solution and the American Planning Association published in 2005 a useful booklet on this subject: *Planning for the Unexpected,* by Laurie Johnson, Laura Samant and Suzanne Frew (Advisory Service Report #531). This guide uses four case study communities to develop a risk management framework for specific risks in governmental entities and to create an effective plan prior to anticipated disasters.

One favorable outcome of *Katrina* (and *Rita*) may be a more intelligent study of potential extreme events and their likelihood and consequences. We need better preparation in the future, requiring the application of the tools of risk management: risk analysis and risk response.

Every catastrophe swamps us with analyses and recommendations. Here are three gleaned from that tidal wave of reaction.

Lessons from *Katrina*

The United States are almost buried, dare I say flooded, by the post-mortems of the 2005 hurricanes, especially *Katrina*. This is as it should be. Failing as badly as we did in that disaster, we should take the time to understand what happened and try and assure the public that, as a society, we can and will do better when the next catastrophe hits. Most recriminations, accusations, legislative posturing, rebuttals and academic blather, however, shed modest light on the situation: we have to dig hard to find some substantive ideas on which it will be worth spending our time and dollars.

I've been sifting through the verbiage looking for those few nuggets, and I think I've found three.

The first is: **Keep in Touch.** Immediately after the shutdown of New Orleans, many employers found it impossible to contact their employees through the traditional methods of the telephone (both wire and wireless) and the postal service. When residents fled to adjacent states, they lost touch with their families, friends and workplaces, exacerbating their economic distress and the abilities of their organizations to revive operations. Business continuity was crippled. Lesson One: we must develop new methods to maintain contacts after major disasters, using email, blogs, websites and more reliable cell phones. A new international organization, Télécoms Sans Frontières, now responds to major catastrophe hits to help distressed families re-establish contact with loved ones. In the future, the loss of telephone communications, the loss of a postal mailing address and the physical dispersion of people across many thousands of miles can be offset by maintaining an organizational website, where employees can find instructions for relief (financial and otherwise), reconstruction and renewal of critical operations. Some companies, including Southwest Airlines, Wal-Mart, Boeing and United Parcel Service, managed to restore some service quickly. A combination of sound planning and continuous communication is the hub of resiliency. Don't depend on outside services!

The second nugget is: **Improvise.** One evening, in an interview on The Newshour, on the Public Broadcasting Service, I heard a notable jazz musician and teacher from New Orleans, Michael White, describe his escape from and return to his city and his current condition. His lesson was, "You have to improvise!" Lovers of New Orleans jazz will understand his point immediately. For his entire musical life he learned how to improvise in jazz, so it was no problem when forced to leave for him to improvise with friends, family and acquaintances. He continues his improvisations after his return.

Improvisation is a learned skill. It requires imagination, the ability to consider a wide range of opportunities and act on those with the most potential benefit. Experience helps, recognizing that improvisation actually works. Finally, it requires both mental and financial resources. Many citizens of New Orleans lacked that last requirement: financial resources, and we continue to learn how badly we mismanaged the distribution of financial aid.

The third nugget is: **Cut your Losses!** The entire southern portion of Louisiana is subsiding into the sea and already a major portion of New Orleans is beneath sea level. New Orleans is a sinking city! The state is losing land at a rate of 25 square miles a year in addition to this subsidence. Add to that ominous forecast three purported consequences of global warming: the slow rise of sea levels, a steady increase in the temperature of ocean waters, and a resulting increase in the frequency and intensity of hurricanes in the Caribbean and the Gulf of Mexico. The entire Gulf Coast of the United States (and similar regions around the world) is a disaster waiting to happen again, and again! As Judith Curry, at Georgia Tech, writes, "Speaking from the climate and environmental-science perspective, a hundred years from now there's just no way there's going to be a city there." We face short-term emotional and political thinking when we consider trying to rebuild even a portion of this city. It's time to consider a radical alternative. If we are successful in the United States we can provide a model for similar regions around the world.

The next time you hear an improvisational Dixieland riff on a clarinet, think of Michael White and the role of improvisation in disaster recovery! Music teaches us a disaster lesson. Think also of how *your* organization will maintain communications with its stakeholders in a disaster, and, finally, think seriously about when to cut your losses!

Our goal must be resilience: the ability of a system to bounce back from a surprise.

CHAPTER 4

Risk and Reputation

> We cannot legislate for the unknown consequences of consequences of consequences.
>
> We must always be aware, never forget, that we may be mistaken.
>
> **Isaiah Berlin, "The Pursuit if the Ideal,"**
> ***The Crooked Timber of Humanity: Chapters in the History of Idea,***
> **Henry Hardy, editor, Vintage Books, New York 1990**

Reputation is an organization's foremost asset, but, as an elusive intangible, it is almost impossible to measure. Not only is reputation subject to change from moment to moment, but also, at any time, "investors" can hold opposite opinions. A shareholder and senior manager can be delighted with a corporation's earnings, related stock price, bonuses and options while, at the same time, some customers are unhappy with prices and services, suppliers disheartened by hard-nosed price squeezes from the corporate buyer a minor employees irate at their meager wages. So what *is* reputation?

Reputation, above all, is a personal perception based on a combination of belief and information, both of which can see radical change from one moment to another. That this "social concept" affects economic results is undeniable, but how do we begin to measure it, much less try and alter perceptions that we think are contrary to what we are trying to achieve? If "reputation" isn't measurable in any conventional sense, does it really exist, as some economists argue? One answer lies in the evidence that organizations enjoying a favorable reputation are given a far longer leash when unpleasantness occurs. Investors and lenders may be willing to give such organizations the benefit of the doubt and even advance more funding. Employees are more likely to stay on the job. Customers will discount the bad news. On the opposite side, when stakeholder confidence turns south, little can be done to save an organization. The collapse of Enron is a perfect example.

Financial institutions have for many years used the "focus group" technique to try and understand how different customers think and react. This permits them to alter their products and services to fit new needs and to offer selective information to enhance the confidence and trust in their organizations. If risk management is a means of anticipating contingencies and developing more coherent responses to protect and enhance reputation, isn't it time that we tried a new approach to *two-way dialogue* in risk management, perhaps along the lines of the familiar focus groups? Not only can we develop better information about possible stakeholder reactions to our risk assessments, but we can also alter our risk responses to build and maintain this essential trust.

Reputation begins with understanding how and what your stakeholders think about an organization. Too often, managers interpret "stakeholders" to mean only shareholders, the Board, and perhaps regulators. The term is far wider than that it includes employees, customers, suppliers, financiers, public officials (beyond just regulators), the media, trade unions, the communities in which an organization operates, and even plaintiff attorneys. And, yes, please add competitors! When a rival in one industry stubs a toe, that misstep reflects also on all its competitors. Each stakeholder set has an "interest," financial, emotional, and intellectual, in an organization and its future. Raising the level of understanding and trust requires an entirely new approach to communications. The old model offered standard periodic "press releases," without any attempt to find out how stakeholders reacted to new information. It was a one-way street: "we will tell you!" Other than the focus group efforts of financial institutions, there was little effort to try and understand the basic feelings of trust and confidence of these different groups. Slowly we are beginning to change this antiquated method.

Here are three sets of suggestions to begin this essential change. The first comes from a 2006 article, the second from a 2005 book, and the third from an Internet success story.

In September 2006, Sophie Gaultier-Gaillard of the Sorbonne and Jean-Paul Louisot, from the CARM Institute, both in Paris, wrote a condensed and cogent piece on reputation risk ("A Positive Approach") in *Strategic Risk* (www.strategicrisk.co.uk). In it the authors proposed thirteen elements of a new and "open" management system required to manage the numerous perceptions that affect reputation. They include:

1. Show active interest in stakeholders, not just shareholders.
2. Use the Internet aggressively. (Be aware of the effects of mention in blogs and learn how to balance those effects.)
3. Create customized information for target groups.
4. Create an open information system that allows different sources to operate and contribute.
5. Report new information continuously, rather than at fixed periods. News affecting an organization never ceases.
6. Develop two-way communication/ exchanges with stakeholders and/or with focus groups representing stakeholders. Listening is more important than telling!

7. Measure performance by a broader range of standards and metrics than the conventional financial ones, including, for example, social responsibility, sustainable development, ethics, etc. This is a difficult suggestion, as many managers remain mesmerized by numbers.
8. Focus on future potential rather than past performance. It isn't your past achievements that count, it is what you can do in the future!
9. Focus more on the "value" created for stakeholders than on "cost-containment." Defining "value" in these terms is a difficult assignment, as we must include both financial and non-financial benefits.
10. Center audits on the quality of processes rather than on mechanical "accounting."
11. Adopt a multicultural and global approach instead of the older national and parochial focus.
12. Re-engineer the business model continuously to reflect global changes. Do not allow it to become static.
13. Adopt a proactive risk management approach, seeking opportunities as well as reducing threats. Do not allow risk management to become the handmaiden of compliance alone!

These thirteen suggestions, if adopted, can help create a new and different and more open structure for risk communication, building reputation.

My second suggestion comes from *Risk Management in Post-Trust Societies,* by Ragnar E. Löfstedt (Palgrave Macmillan, New York, 2005). How do we communicate the relativities of risk assessments and responses when we live in a society that distrusts most institutions? That is the problem that Professor Löfstedt addresses in this short but provocative book. In the past twenty years our faith and trust in governments, corporations and religious and other nonprofit institutions have been corroded, after countless examples of fraud, mendacity and outright criminal behavior. Add to this the new immediacy of information, the concentration of political power and the "amplification of risk by the media," and we have a situation in which disbelief is the automatic first reaction to any public comment! How then can we develop new means of risk communication to help "minimize disputes, resolve issues and anticipate problems before they result in an irreversible breakdown in communications?"

I have encouraged increased two-way dialogue with stakeholders as one means of improving trust and confidence, but Löfstedt argues that this is not necessarily the "be-all and end-all of risk management." He makes a convincing caution. While this book is addressed primarily to public policy risk managers and regulators, its ideas are equally applicable to the profit making and nonprofit sectors.

The author begins with four key premises:

(1) Regulation is essential,
(2) Regulatory bodies need to have public trust,

(3) Public trust in regulatory bodies is vulnerable, uneven, and may be declining overall, and,
(4) We need to re-examine the use of various risk management tools.

He then tests nine conceptual ideas involving the level of perceived public trust and the nature of risk situations against four case studies, finding that in some circumstances, deliberative communication can be "expensive and time-consuming" without sufficient benefits to warrant its use. In some cases ("high distrust") "charismatic individuals are more helpful in negotiating successful deliberative outcomes." The four cases involve the siting of a waste incinerator in the North Black Forest of Germany, the re-licensing of four International Paper hydro-electric dams on the Androscoggin River in Maine, a post-incident study of a nuclear accident at the Barsebäck nuclear power plant in Sweden in 1992, and, finally, the well-known situation involving the decision of Shell to attempt to dump its oil storage buoy, Brent Spar, in the North Sea in 1995.

In the International Paper hydro-dam re-licensing, the author made a telling comment: "the process almost completely excluded lawyers who could have increased the lack of trust in the regulatory process as a whole and would have inevitably increased the costs as well." How true, but how often is it possible to exclude them?

His summary:

— In a high public trust environment, extensive direct public deliberation will not be needed.
— In a low public trust environment, deliberation in the form of special interest groups or publics, technocrats in the form of experts or scientists, or economists, (are) necessary. The extent of their involvement in the policy-making process depends on the reasons for public distrust.
— Involving interest groups in the policy-making process because of impartiality is a risky process, and may increase public distrust.

Professor Löfstedt opens new areas for discussion in risk communication, and I hope that others will follow his lead for the profit-making sector.

My third suggestion for improving risk communication comes from the Internet. Many are familiar with the astounding success and relative accuracy of the website Wikipedia, a virtual encyclopedia open to anyone for addition, deletion or correction. If we are really intent on opening the lines of risk assessment communication, it occurs to me that in Wikipedia we have an opportunity to expand risk dialogue within an organization. Many organizations produce "riskmaps" and "dashboards" as techniques of distributing and explaining useful information about the relative status of risks at any time. Unfortunately, as soon as we produce them they are out of date. The question: how to keep them current?

The answer lies in *continual input* from all employees. I therefore propose that every organization start its own *Riskipedia*. Those responsible for risk assessments should post on an intranet a summary of the data used to create the likelihood, consequence and timing distributions, including their graphs of positive and negative outcomes. They should then ask everyone in the organization to review these summaries using their own continuing experience, adding their own comments and data as necessary. In time the organization will experience two benefits: a significant increase in the awareness of different risks by everyone plus additional intelligent input of unusual and unexpected outcomes, plus and minus, enabling the risk analysts to modify their projections. It will become a cross-pollination of stakeholder perceptions.

The idea of an open risk assessment website may be a shock to some who prefer to hold their knowledge privately and confidentially, but, in this new era of transparent information, the advantages could outweigh the disadvantages. Bill Durodie, a senior lecturer on risk and corporate security at Cranfield University, recently said, "my thesis is that once people stop participating in formal and informal networks, they become on the whole more isolated and when you are on your own you start to feel more insecure" (*Business Insurance Europe,* October 9, 2006). Understanding and participating in the creation of risk assessments, through a riskipedia, should enhance corporate security.

Should a riskipedia be expanded to include representatives of external stakeholders?

There is a model for this idea of a riskipedia. The Environmental Protection Agency of the U. S. Government maintains IRIS, the Integrated Risk Information Service, at *www.epa.gov/iris*. It is a summary of the EPA estimates of health hazards from exposure to many different chemical substances. Its "users" now are worldwide: federal agencies, chemical producers, labor unions, state and local officials, regulators in other countries, lawyers, universities and quangos. While most of these users simply download information, I suspect there will be a time in the future when this site will become more like Wikipedia, allowing comment and input from other sources. For further analysis of IRIS, see the three letters to the editor in *Risk Analysis,* Vol. 26, No. 6, 2006.

The real value of a riskipedia is providing information to those who can best learn from and use it. Too often we remain constrained by the archaic idea of "the need to know," limiting distribution of useful information. Or we think that we must protect "proprietary information" from the prying eyes of competitors, when in fact, it is entirely possible for different observers to create simultaneously the same inventions and ideas. Or extra-cautious lawyers advise us to say nothing, post nothing, for fear of legal action. Nonsense!

Our major problem is our overwhelming ignorance of historical data and experience, even as the Internet opens doors to global information. John Skar, of Massachusetts Mutual, in Springfield, recently noted to me the four levels of historical ignorance we must combat:

1. Unawareness of past events
2. Awareness of events, but a lack of intelligence and perspective to draw comparisons
3. Awareness of events and patterns, but denial about current similarities; and
4. Awareness of events, patterns and similarities, but an unwillingness to act because of political or religious agendas.

True, we may never overcome all these obstacles, but an active riskipedia could help surmount some of them.

So some new forms of risk communication are required to enhance the confidence and trust of stakeholders in any organization, that "reputation" so essential to future success. Our French authors suggest thirteen steps to a new and more open approach to relaying risk assessments and risk responses. The Swedish author warns that communication *per se* may not be the total answer, and, finally, I suggest that we should explore the idea of a riskipedia.

CHAPTER 5

Population, Fundamentalism and Climate Change

> I am arguing not against change, but for a modest, tentative, and skeptical acceptance of it.
>
> **Edward Tenner, *Why Things Bite Back: Technology and the Revenge of Unintended Consequences,* Alfred A. Knopf, New York 1996**

I wrote the following piece while sweltering in uncommon Maine heat.

The Frog and Boiling Water

I'm sitting in my attic office in Maine in late July, on a summer afternoon. I've been writing for three hours and, suddenly, I realize that I'm oozing sweat. The temperature is near 100 degrees Fahrenheit in this uninsulated garret on a windless day. It reminds me of the story of the frog and boiling water: put a frog in a tub of boiling water and he'll jump out immediately, but put him in a tub of cool water and turn the heat up, and he'll sit there and boil to death!

Just so! Ours is a natural tendency to respond to the apparent sudden change, even as we disregard or discount those modest, creeping alterations. We ignore continued warnings of boiling to death. Risk officers are no different. How many have taken seriously two creeping risks that will affect us in the next fifty years? One, of course, is population growth. We've read about it. We've heard the forecasters. Chicken Littles since Malthus have bemoaned our fate. But have we developed any concrete responses designed to assure the longevity of our organizations? The population of the United States hit 300 million in October 2006. This earth's population is 6.5 billion and may reach as high as 9 billion by the second half of this century. Then, if we are lucky, population reproduction rates may sink to 2.1 children per couple or lower. This rate is already in evidence in some countries in Europe, in Japan and close to it in North America. An end to the rapid escalation of population could mean an easing of the pressures on natural resources, even if this brings temporary economic disruptions. At the same time, we could sustain major population reductions if we cannot solve such potential problems as pandemics and genocidal warfare. On the other side, if we are successful in attacking AIDS, influenza, malaria and tuberculosis with some of the new funds from the Gates Foundation, we may find ourselves with millions of younger people who need to be fed, clothed and employed. The "ifs" are imponderable! Nonetheless, we should spend serious time considering the possibilities.

A second "creeping" exposure is the rising level of the world's seas. Imperceptibility is also its characteristic. In the last century, environmentalists report that global sea levels have risen about eight inches. Living here in Maine with a twice daily change of tide of almost ten feet, it's difficult to see the four inches of reported change in the fifty years I've been here. But climate change, we are told, accelerating the melting of icecaps, may amplify the rise to 20 inches in 20 years, and if Greenland and Antarctica lose more of their ice, we could see a rise of 20 *feet* or more. Here in Maine, with a house that is perched only 25 feet above mean high water, I'd notice that!

We tend to disregard slow, incremental changes naturally incorporated into our systems. Before these seemingly consistent creeps start moving more rapidly in one direction or another, it is time to pay attention. Population and sea levels challenge us. Don't be a frog! Consider imperceptibility

In January 2007, I commented on three of the major risk issues facing all organizations.

Issues in Uncertainty

That's exactly the problem! We face so many different "issues" in uncertainty during the next twelve months that we may settle only for those risks we think we know and understand. That could be a serious mistake. It's time to look beyond our comfort zones.

The "conventional" risks still remain as daunting. How will our credit predictions pan out in the face of potential recessions in North America and Europe and the noisy, noxious exhalation of the real estate bubble? What will happen to the market for the U.S. dollar, especially if the Chinese re-value the yuan? If Asians, and others, decide to shift their investments into other currencies, will the Federal Reserve increase interest rates, reclaiming foreign cash but stimulating a domestic downslide? Where are the opportunities in a devalued dollar? In the regulatory arena, what will be the effects of Basel II, Solvency II, and the possible softening of Sarbanes-Oxley? How will shareholders and regulators respond to mounting evidence of excessive executive remuneration, especially those notorious backdated options for officers and directors? What can or should risk officers do about the problem? What are the unintended consequences of misplaced financial incentives? What damage (or opportunities) can we expect from this year's sequence of hurricanes, typhoons, floods, tsunamis, and tornadoes? How many employees will be injured on the job? Will their pensions deteriorate further? What about the mounting caseload of litigation? These organizational uncertainties are more than enough to keep us busy in 2007. Many of them can be translated into risk (a range of likely occurrences and consequences) from amassed data and past experience, allowing us to plan a bit more intelligently for most outcomes. Alone they crowd and could dominate our agenda for the next twelve months.

Surrounding this thicket of conventional organizational uncertainty, however, are global concerns of greater importance. These are the systemic, long-term trends that influence everyone, worldwide. A single organization can seldom affect these risks in any material way, and too often groups and governments are both ineffective and slow to act. Yet they are the issues that, I suggest, should be on the top of this year's risk management list.

What are these global concerns? In the early 1990s, I suggested a sequence of the major "global" and strategic risks that submerge the more mundane "organizational" or tactical risks on which we spend so much of our time. My "risk spectrum" suggests that most of us spend too little time on these global issues and too much on the tactical or organizational. One reason is that most of us are trained to look at the specific, not the general. That's our comfort range. Another is that we sense that there is little we can do to change the situation, so we simply follow the crowd and look elsewhere. A third is that our boards and senior managers insist on performance in the near-term, not the long-term. We tacitly acknowledge the global issues but do little about them.

So this year of 2007, I focus on three of these "global" risks, arguing that they deserve as much time of risk officers as the more traditional organizational ones. PricewaterhouseCoopers argued this point in its December, 2006, paper, "Enterprise Risk Management: Making It Over the Hurdle," when it pressed for an "initiative to extend beyond litigation and operational risks to a wider range of global risks."

In my "spectrum" diagram, I listed six issues: climate change, political fragmentation, pandemics, population change/aging, nuclear proliferation, and religious fundamentalism. That their importance hasn't changed in the past 15 years is confirmation of their significance. They are also closely interconnected. Each one affects the others, requiring a combined analysis. As an example, concerns about climate change push governments to re-assess nuclear power, leading to the proliferation of nuclear power and, inevitably, of nuclear weapons.

Another example is the attempt by the United States and a few isolated allies to change the culture and governance of the Middle East and, with it, perhaps the entire Islamic world. Already this attempt is acknowledged to be an "unmitigated disaster," (the description of Hendrik Hertzberg in *The New Yorker,* December 18, 2007). It places the world's richest and most militarily powerful country in a position where almost any further action will create even more regional chaos, whose effects will be felt worldwide. As a result, each organization must redraw its risk scenarios and analyses to consider these effects. This coalition action has already stimulated religious fundamentalism, stirred renewed interest in nuclear weapons, and wasted funds that could have been better spent on health and climate improvement. Above all, the Iraq war will probably create further political fragmentation.

The relationships of global events and situations are easy to map. Take, as an example, three of my interconnected global risks: climate change, population change and religious fundamentalism. I argue that the issue of **population**, its growth, change and aging, transcends all others. *It is the defining moral, political and economic issue of our times and our future.* The human species totaled 6.5 billion in 2005. How many more can this earth handle? While birth rates have dropped below replacement levels in Europe and Japan, they remain explosive in Africa, South America, and many parts of Asia. Indonesians are increasing by 1.3% a year, meaning that they will count 30 million more people in less than 45 years. The United States hit 300 million in 2006 and will count 400 million *in less than 40 years*, the result of both immigration and a higher birth rate for some segments of society. The dire forecasts of Thomas Malthus have so far been wrong, but some argue that we may, after all, reach that point in global population when our numbers exceed this earth's tolerance in terms of food, water, energy, and the degradation of fragile ecosystems. We read almost daily of problems created by a growing population in some parts of the world, a shrinking one in others (the geriatric "bubble" in Europe, Japan and North America), and an increasing mobile one trying to immigrate to more favorable climes and economies (in the United States, people are moving to the southwestern states, where already we have too little water to support those there). Political inertia and social forces of myth and superstition combine to cripple efforts to attack the population problem. At the same time, we devote enormous amounts of money, both philanthropic and governmental, to reducing death rates from poverty and such diseases as malaria, tuberculosis and AIDS. If effective, our success will further increase population.

In the developed world, where the birth rate has fallen, we face economic disruption. The bubble of an aging population in Europe, North America and Japan can easily bankrupt existing social security systems unless we take immediate and radical corrective action. Waves of illegal immigration from other nations and legal movement within countries can disrupt corporate employment and planning. The raids on Swift & Co. plants in the United States in December 2006 prove that both reputation and legal problems result from failure to understand these issues

That brings us to the second of these three intertwined problems: **religious fundamentalism**. Increasing religious polarization and mutual intolerance undermine efforts to combat population issues. We now live in a period of loud religious revival, in which priests, imams, rabbis and other gurus tell us to discard reason, to allow them to interpret the world for us, and to excoriate if not physically eliminate infidels and non-believers. They preach irrational intolerance to protect their own narrow fiefdoms. The rampant resort to terrorism in the Middle East, India, Sri Lanka, Africa, Asia, and, yes, even in Europe and North America, is a result of this religious resurgence. Some argue it is their last gasp of outmoded thinking before they succumb to rationality. The Talibanization of Islam is a disease that infects other religions as well. Too often religious leaders interfere directly with proposed population solutions such as enhanced family planning, the use of condoms to restrain childbirth as well as reduce disease, and stem cell research. Much of this reactionary resistance comes from thinking submerged in centuries-old myths concocted by desert tribesmen to protect their nomadic cultures. Very simply, conditions have changed dramatically from 2000 years ago. When doubt and curiosity are stifled, as some many of the religious fundamentalists preach, then our innate human ability to solve problems is equally suppressed. Fyodor Dostoyevsky expressed it well in *The Brothers Karamazov*:

— "Stupidity is brief and guileless, while reason hedges and hides. Reason is a scoundrel, stupidity is direct and honest."
— ". . . only three powers on earth, (are) capable of conquering and holding captive forever the conscience of these feeble rebels, for their own happiness—these powers are miracle, mystery, and authority." (The latter quote is from the Grand Inquisitor, and both are from the Richard Pevear/Larissa Volokhonsky translation, Farrar, Strauss and Giroux, New York, 2002)

Religious fundamentalism is a pandemic that has already infected large portions of this earth. Its effects will continue to be felt for many years to come. It refuses to die quickly.

That brings me to the third of these three connected issues, **climate change**. This subject is already high on the agenda of many organizations. Some managers practice "triple-bottom-line" reporting and others create "social responsibility indices." But how much of this represents real effort and how much lip service to enhance reputation? In 2006 alone new publicity advanced understanding of the issue. We watched Al Gore's film, *An Inconvenient Truth,* a dramatic visual summary of our deteriorating situation. We read E. O. Wilson's plea for maintaining biological diversity in *The Creation*, Sir Nicholas Stern's October 2006 analysis of the economics of warming, *The Economist's* climate survey of September 9, 2006, Elizabeth Kolbert's warning about the effects on our oceans in "The Darkening Sea," in the November 20 issue of *The New Yorker*, and Dan Anderson's plea for "sustainability" in *Corporate Survival: The Critical Importance of Sustainability Risk Management* (published late in 2005). We agree we will experience "major disruptions to economic and social activity, later in this century and in the next, on a scale similar to those associated with the great wars and the economic depression of the first half of the 20th century," (from the Stern Report). Some, however, still question how much we should spend to change the trend, if we can indeed change the trend as quickly as we think, and how much of the trend is attributable to natural change compared to human pollution. Philip Conkling expressed this difficulty well in a column called "Global Warming—Fact or Hoax?" in the August 2006 issue of *Working Waterfront:* " . . . there is no proof of cause and effect because the physical mechanisms that control the global climate system are mind-numbingly complex and thus not completely understood." But, he went on, "a basic feature of human intelligence is our ability to generalize patterns from particular experiences." Therein lies our hope. We face, as *The Economist* wrote, a "cascade of uncertainties," not only in our assessments of future conditions but also in what we can and should do as individuals, organizations and governments. Climate change *is* happening but where should we spend our limited funds? Bjorn Lomborg argues that argues that allocating too much to carbon dioxide reduction is both expensive and of limited effect. He suggests using the same funds to improve the lot of residents of underdeveloped countries, those who are likely to be most affected by temperature changes, droughts and flooding, to enhance their ability to adapt and move. But Lomborg's prescription may lead to an even larger population! Which way should we go? The tools of risk management can play a significant role is making better decisions.

Andrew R. B. Ferguson wrote a compelling comment on the Gore film in early October (see *www.populationmedia.org*, one of the best sites for population and related information). He listed five additional "inconvenient truths" to the "global warming" of the film. Each one indicates the difficulty surrounding any response to this risk.

1. The "immense difficulty of replacing fossil fuels." Both nuclear (fission and fusion) plus solar energy are options but we face huge technological problems if either or both are to replace our dependence on fossil fuels.
2. A decrease in fossil fuel usage in the West (targeted at "an improbable 60%") will probably be cancelled by a "probable 130% increase" in China, India and Indonesia (a trend exacerbated by population growth in these countries).
3. Any "per capita emission reduction" in developed nations will be slow.
4. Economic globalization is a "powerful driver for fossil fuel consumption."
5. And perhaps most importantly, Ferguson suggests we need to change the "belief of economists and the commercial world" in the idea of "continuing growth." We must implant the idea that "the capitalist system works reasonably well without growth" as its dominant idea.

This "growth fetish," including the population one nurtured by too many religious leaders fearful of the loss of "customers," may well require another century to correct, but, as Ferguson says, we need an "immense reduction in population if everyone is to live even moderately well."

Of course, if we fail to take specific action, yet another "inconvenient truth" may appear: the human species may manage to control its own numbers through losses from pandemics and starvation, leading ultimately to the development of a genetic disposition to fewer, not more, children. Darwin may yet be proved right again. But think of the cost and pain of that particular evolution!

Climate change *is* taking place and it *is* probable that it will materially affect *homo sapiens* and all other species inhabiting this earth. The growth of our particular species is probably the single-most significant factor contributing to this change and it is therefore surprising that so few have suggested we try and alter our birthrates. That we have not done so can also be attributed to the regressive ignorance of many of the world's leading religions. So all three global risk issues come back together.

I conclude by encouraging risk officers to put these global risk issues on top of their agendas, even though their assessments and suggested responses are both flawed and modest. These issues will truly affect our lives, as individuals and organizations. The plethoras of organizational risks we are so comfortable managing are relatively insignificant.

Perhaps, just perhaps, understanding the nature of these uncertainties and learning to live with them will enhance our management skills. Jason Elliot believed this to be the case, as he wrote in *An Unexpected Light,* his 1998 story of a walk across Afghanistan, then operating under the Taliban:

— "I had given up on earlier and more ambitious schemes and was prepared to make an ally of uncertainty, which with luck so often finds a partnership."
— "I wanted to be free, if only for a day, of the tyranny of knowing what to expect in advance; to ride, in effect, a high wave of uncertainty until I could no longer feel its motion."

CHAPTER 6

Gambling and Litigation: A Connection?

I wrote this commentary in 1994 for Focus Number 11, *published by Zurich Insurance Company, on one of the world's most pervasive and destructive habits. I've added a few minor updates, but, in 2007, the problem is, if anything, worse.*

Is it a coincidence that the problem of excessive litigation in the United States seems to have started about the same time as the resurgence in gambling? Both aberrations were only modest problems in the early 1960s, and both have exploded creating serious concerns about societal change. The United States now seems to be a society that not only *wants* but also *expects* "something for nothing," a common attitude of gamblers. When things go awry, we search for someone to blame and to sue. We are unable to accept personal responsibility for our own actions or acknowledge that certain events are truly "accidental," the responsibility of no one. We are susceptible to the lure of the "pot of gold," the "quick fix," and the "get-rich scheme."

In a similar vein, we want balanced federal and State budgets but we are unwilling to reduce expenses or raise taxes. We demand health care for everyone but complain about the cost, expecting magic solutions that impose no financial burden on us. The rest of the world looks on in horror and incredulity as we launch a tidal wave of lawsuits, clogging the courts and adding a layer of costs threatening to render many of our products and services non-competitive in world trade. How much of this litigious behavior can be attributed to a gambling mentality that has infiltrated out psyche, staring with our willingness to permit legal lotteries in 1964?

Gambling is hardly new to the American scene. Lotteries helped pay for part of the costs of the American Revolutionary War. Casinos and riverboat gambling flourished after the Civil War. We even bet on which Calaveras County, California, frog could out-jump others. But each burst of gambling activity has been followed by an equally strong political, social and religious backlash, as our engrained Puritan ethic re-established itself. Gambling lost its respectability and was then suppressed for many years until its next resurgence. Is it possible that we are again at the peak of just such a cyclical resurgence?

The current cycle started with the approval of the first state lottery in New Hampshire in 1964. State lotteries spread rapidly thereafter and legalized gambling is now a major business in the United States. According to one source, the gambling industry accounts for over $300 billion annually, of which about ten percent is attributable to casino gambling. Its advocates try to con us by substituting the euphemism "gaming" for the other term. The gambling business thrives in all states but two (Utah and Hawaii) in the form of racetrack betting (dogs and horses), casinos, gambling on Indian reservations, bingo, and the lotteries in 37 states. Today this legalized gambling is strongly supported by both politicians and religious organizations, in contrast to their strident opposition of past years, since to both the proceeds appear to be a relatively easy way to generate funds for arguably beneficial services. But what are the costs of gambling? How much is being wasted on a non-creative infrastructure? What are the short-term and long-term costs to individuals and society of psychological addition to gambling?

And what about litigation? Suing your neighbor, a corporation, or government, once treated as scandalous a behavior as gambling, is now as acceptable a way of life as the daily betting trains to Atlantic City and the come-ons luring gamblers to Las Vegas. People openly boast about successful lawsuits in which they have won large awards. A lawsuit is now considered an opportunity to grab the brass ring and retire.

Is there a connection or is it simply coincidence? My suspicion is that there is a causal connection between the two developments, although it may take years of academic diagnosis to confirm it. Over the past thirty years we have witnessed an erosion of civility and mutual respect. We have also seen the social degradation in the rise of the "me" decade (the 1980s), when "looking out for No. 1" (the name of a best selling book) became the dominant practice. This morphed into the belief that "greed is good," exemplified by the film character Gordon Gecko in the 1990s and the outrageous pay packages of executives. That all of this led to excessive litigation is hardly surprising, as pompous trial lawyers brought class action suits on behalf of the "little people," only to stuff their own pockets with millions. Driving this tidal wave have been such practices as contingency fees, the easy option of class-action suits, rulings of "joint and several liability," and, perhaps worst of all, the manifestations of ambulance chasing on the part of aggressive attorneys seeking clients following disasters. Speculative suits crowd dockets, delaying justice.

We can't really blame the lawyers. They simply followed and participated in this feeding frenzy. We now have more lawyers per capita of population than most developed nations (the per capita rates are higher in Singapore and Pakistan, but I suspect these are anomalies). Similarly, we can't blame the insurance companies. They too followed the flow. Where once liability insurance was considered to be against public policy, in that its availability might lead persons and organizations to act less responsibly, today it is often the most expensive piece of a corporate insurance program. For some professionals, liability insurance and allied risk financing can run more than 15% of annual revenues. Medical malpractice liability insurance costs have run physicians out of practice. Product, professional, and environmental liability insurance suffer periodic crises in which costs escalate and availability declines, along with demands that "government must do something." Nonetheless our litigation habit supports a considerable part of a non-life insurance business whose premiums are on a par with the global gambling trade. It's hard to see how either or both could be realistically reduced or dismantled.

The blame for this mess falls squarely on us. Our attitudes changed in the past fifty years and today we tolerate, even encourage, that which we despised years ago.

Yet can we legitimately find a connection between the rise of gambling and the almost simultaneous rise in litigation? Is it just a coincidence? I doubt it. The American love-hate relationship with risk, with the roll of the dice, seems to be too strong. It has manifested itself in the joint rise of these two social aberrations, as we try to beat the "system" and "the house." In both gambling and litigation, the overhead expenses are horrific, a fact we cannot overlook. For the billions of dollars sucked into the legal maw each year, less than 30% reach the pockets of the injured parties, leaving the "system" of the courts, attorneys (plaintiff *and* defense), insurance companies, and regulators all sucking away our money. Gambling is hardly more efficient, given the interest and avarice of organized crime and the notable bumblings of governmental bureaucracies.

I argue the connection between gambling and litigation perhaps because I am an optimist and because an academic has raised a ray of hope. Nelson Rose, a gambling expert and law professor at the Whittier Law School in Los Angeles, suggests that our gambling craze may be peaking, as it has done before, and that society may be moving toward more rational behavior. His prediction for the next demise of gambling, when we will view it as socially unacceptable, is 2029. That's a rather precise date, but I'll accept it! But if this demise does take place, will it also include a shift away from litigious behavior as well? Dr. Rose's magical year is still many years away, leaving plenty of time for lawyers to get rich, for organizations to be throttle by senseless litigation, and for insurance companies to be drowned in claims. But if you agree that there is some causal connection between gambling and litigation, you may, as I do, find a glimmer of optimism!

Perhaps we may return to a day in which we accept responsibility for our own actions, if indeed such a day ever existed. Or we may progress to a new plane of altruism for the misfortunes of others. Do you remember the Amish reaction to a barn fire in the 19th century? The farmer's neighbors would gather immediately to help him rebuild his barn. While some socio-biologists counter that this is only evidence of enlightened self-interest, others, such as Harvard's Edward O. Wilson and Sloan-Kettering's Lewis Thomas, argue that we have a genetic streak of altruism within us, despite our "marked hereditary predisposition to aggressive behavior" (Wilson, *On Human Nature,* Harvard University Press, 1978, and Thomas, *Lives of a Cell,* Viking Press, 1974). We see signs of generous human responses to catastrophes, ranging from Hurricane Andrew (1993) and the Northridge Earthquake (1994) to the Indonesian tsunami of 2005. Is there a way of encouraging this altruistic behavior while discouraging the bad habits of gambling and excessive litigation?

If, as Dr. Rose suggest, the current gambling mania subsides by the end of the first quarter of this century, will it affect litigation as well? I hope so.

CHAPTER 7

A Contrarian's View of Insurance

I wrote the first paper in 1994, shortly after I retired from full-time management consulting, full of years of frustration about an insurance industry seemingly incapable of progress and about the insurance buyers who called themselves "risk managers," equally chained to their insurance vendor masters. Eleven years later, in 2005, following the disclosures of broker malfeasance under Eliot Spitzer, the Attorney General of New York State, I wrote the second paper, published in Business Insurance. *Nothing seems to have changed, and late in 2006, some of the brokers who first gave up contingency commissions, were back in the game, with the approval of regulatory authorities! A dinosaur, the non-life insurance industry, with its leeches, its agents, brokers and other intermediaries clinging to its sides, continues to stumble into the future, perhaps awaiting the asteroid that inevitably must come and crush it. This chapter ends with a 2007 comment.*

> . . . there is no nonsense so gross that society will not, at some time, make a doctrine of it and defend it with every weapon of communal stupidity.
>
> **Robertson Davies, *The Cunning Man*, Viking Press, New York 1994**

1994 Paper: A Contrarian's View

Some years ago, as a schoolboy, I traveled to Boston to hear a new play by Christopher Fry, *The Lady's Not for Burning.* From it I remember a line that serves as my theme. Thomas Mendip, the hero, laments that "the moon is nothing but a circumambulating aphrodisiac divinely subsidized to provoke the world into a rising birth rate." Almost a Malthusian thought, it is hardly the definition of a scientist or a romantic. It is rather the view of a skeptic, even a cynic. And that is my note: it is time to look more skeptically at both the global insurance industry and its related risk management discipline so that we can reform and recreate them to meet the challenges of the next few decades.

I look at an insurance industry that, in large measure, fails to meet the needs of it larger organizational customers in Europe and the United States and at risk management practitioners who equally fail to meet the needs of their organizations. Both risk becoming redundant. I suggest that a skeptical, contrarian's view of the current situation is required to help us move responsibly into the future. Above all, I hope these comments will serve as stimuli for discussion and action.

Much of the current problem, I'm afraid, derives from an antiquated view of the nature and value of insurance as a risk-financing tool. Zen Buddhism for centuries has used the koan as a means of freeing one's mind from conventional thought. A koan is a brief statement or question, seemingly incomprehensible or unanswerable that, when thoroughly considered helps break one's mind out of the traps of experience and tradition. Perhaps the most famous koan is the question, "What is the sound of one hand clapping?" We need a few similar mind-expanding questions to break the chains of convention binding insurance and insurance risk management. I tried my first in 1971 at a meeting of the directors of a major insurance brokerage firm, when I challenged them with the idea that "insurance is nothing more than a pre-funded line of credit." It is *not* a unique financial product: it is part of a spectrum of financial tools, very similar to those found in banking. Even today, many insurance risk managers cannot accept this statement. I tried my second koan-like idea in 1985: "There is no such thing as risk transfer; there is only risk sharing." This is more challenging and fewer managers subscribe to it, even though I believe that it will become the central theme in future risk financing.

As we move through the apparent failures of the present and the possibilities for the future, please keep in mind Thomas Mendip's skeptical definition of the moon and my two koan-like challenges. They serve as *leitmotifs* for change.

Where is the insurance industry failing today's global organizations?

It balks at risk. Too often insurers respond to new risk situations with a barrage of exclusions, limit reductions, premium increases, and outright cancellations. Examples abound in the United States including the bumps and grinds in environmental liability, medical malpractice liability, and governmental liability. It isn't as if these risks are unfundable. Beginning with the medical malpractice crisis of the mid-1970s, doctors and hospitals were forced to create their own insurance companies and trusts when the conventional insurance industry simply bailed out. Today these entities account for over 60% of medical malpractice premiums. They are financially strong. They have developed innovative risk controls. And above all they have the confidence and support of their owners, something that commercial insurers seldom have. Similarly, local governments found it difficult to obtain, first, workers' compensation insurance, and later liability insurance, in cascading crises in the 1970s and 1980s. Today governments operate 430 risk sharing pools in the United States, providing a wide range of covers, serving 43% of all governmental bodies. The premiums in these pools were $1.2 billion in 1988, rising to $5.5 billion in 1992. These are premiums that otherwise might have flowed to conventional insurers had they not been so risk averse.

And what of the newer risks? What has the insurance industry done to respond to investment risks (hedges, swaps, options and futures)? What has it done to offer imaginative covers for political and regulatory risks? I fear the industry remains mired in trying to underwrite the risks of the past, and even there it operates poorly. Shaun Wilkinson, the risk manager of New Zealand's Fletcher Challenge Limited, laments the non-availability of both limits and covers: "Amid many layers of fillers and contortions (e.g. intermediaries, insurers, reinsurers), is it any wonder that the buyer often ends up with a bicycle rather than the Sherman tank that he really needs?"

It is unstable. In the past, the payment of an insurance premium meant certain smaller costs to reduce some larger uncertain costs in the future. Today, the volatility of the insurance market—premiums and covers—seems to many financial officers to be more a roller coaster ride than a stable platform. In addition, close analyses of insurer financial statements reveal a disquieting insecurity. Investment firms suggest that many non-life (property/casualty) insurers in the United States may be as much as 20% under-reserved. Catastrophes, such as windstorms and earthquakes, could conceivably cripple the non-life industry. And environmental liability continues to loom as a potential disaster in and of itself. Insurers, even after recent catastrophes, take too little of their own risk compared to their surpluses, preferring an over-reliance on reinsurance. Since the reliability of reinsurance is itself suspect, some observers believe that the industry is building another risk spiral, comparable to the LMX spiral in London, one which could see it disintegrate into falling dominoes. The explosion of potential losses from major natural disasters has led the industry to beg for relief from government in the form of excess protection, another sign of instability. In fairness, I must admit that the industry lacks something it needs in most jurisdiction, the ability to set aside catastrophe reserves on a tax deferred basis.

It is poorly managed Insurance has dropped precipitously in public esteem, for numerous reasons. It is seemingly incapable of delivering quotations and policies on time or invoices accurately. It often treats its customers as if they are dishonest when a claim is filed, thus creating a self-fulfilling prophecy as customers respond in anger with legal counsel. Its handling of disclosures of dishonesty has been clumsy, witness the recent Metropolitan Life and Prudential Securities settlements in the United States. When a large loss occurs, it may force its insured to sue for recovery of otherwise legitimate funds. It uses archaic tools for measurement of performance and comparisons, and it has perpetuated unconscionably high expenses in a day and age of cost cutting in other industries. An expense ratio over 30% is completely irrational when compared to other financial services. It continues to be overly insulated from its customers by its distribution systems, systems that date back to the nineteenth century. The industry fails to attract the brightest and best from leading universities and graduate schools, and this has allowed mediocrity to grow over time. And finally the industry is politically inept. It prefers to fight rear-guard actions to protect its turf rather than sponsor progressive initiatives to promote regulations that could help build a more modern and responsive risk financing system. In the United States it continues to prefer a system of chaotic regulation by the fifty states to a more rational and less costly national one. And its lack of political clout means that the industry cannot obtain the relief that it most needs: tax deferral for catastrophe funding.

It is losing to competition. In part because of all these failings, the non-life insurance industry, particularly in the United States, is losing out to new competitors. Over the past twenty years its own customers, the larger insurance buyers, have singly and jointly created more than 3,000 captive insurance companies to handle their own risks. These companies account for $14 billion in premiums, $30 billion in assets, and $13.5 billion in surplus. This is about 6% of the total non-life premiums from Europe and North America. When government pools, self-insurance (deductibles and deliberate non-purchase of coverage), and alternative risk financing are taken into account, I suspect that these non-conventional—insurance techniques account for more than 40% of total risk financing for commercial, governmental and nonprofit organizations. If it isn't enough that its own customers are taking huge bites out of its market share, the insurance industry is now beginning to lose out to banks, credit card companies and even telephone companies. Its response has been to try and hold back the flood with laws and regulations, but buyers are moving en masse to alternatives. The waters are now threatening to engulf the industry.

At the same time, the buying organizations have their own problems. Where are insurance risk managers failing their own organizations?

They over-focus on insurance. Faced with numerous new risks and opportunities to expand their responsibilities, most insurance risk managers have restricted their views to the narrow field of insurance and claims. They have been aided and abetted by some academic institutions that continue to teach that there is a difference between "pure" and "speculative" risk, a dichotomy that was effectively discredited years ago. What this outmoded idea has done is continue an "insurance" silo within an organization, one increasingly disconnected with all other operations. Risk is the compound estimate of the probable frequency, severity and public perception of unexpected events. It does not have artificial academic boundaries, despite the fact that by so doing professors can more easily train their students for future jobs in the insurance business. As a result of too narrow a focus, most insurance managers have missed opportunities to apply the risk management discipline to newly developing risks such as foreign exchange, interest rates, credit, derivatives, compliance, plus political and regulatory change. Others now step into the breach. And they are the ones who now take the title "risk manager," witness recent articles in *The Economist* and *Business Week,* and the advertisements of banking and investment firms.

They have missed service opportunities. Insurance risk managers are seldom known for their expertise in risk assessment and risk control. Too often they have ceded such work to insurance companies, insurance brokers, and consultants, rather than build expertise internally. More often others within the organization have developed innovative risk assessment and control mechanisms, plus tools for risk communication with stakeholders. Similarly, too few insurance risk managers have offered to take charge of contingency or disaster planning programs, allowing others to fill this gap. As a result, there is a lack of coordination among the internal and external providers of these services.

They are married to their vendors. In most cases, insurance risk managers depend heavily on the services of brokers and insurers, spending an inordinate amount of time in the process of selecting and supervising them, often changing as frequently as once a year. Some "professional" association meetings, like the annual conference of the Risk & Insurance Management Society, are carnivals of expensive exhibit booths, handouts, hospitality suites and lavish entertainment. They appear to have prostituted themselves to their vendors, since they are incapable of or unwilling to finance their own activities. Even England's prestigious Institute of Risk Management is not immune. Of fifteen annual prizes offered by IRM, thirteen are named for and sponsored by vendors. Over time, of course, this dependence corrupts the alleged professionalism of those who prefer to be called "risk managers."

Obviously, there are many notable exceptions to these skeptical and caustic comments, but unfortunately they simply prove my generalizations. Have I overstated them? Perhaps, but we need a shock to our system to challenge our thinking.

The Needs of the Future

It is axiomatic that we live in a world of increasing uncertainty. In the past, we were seldom bothered by things we did not know, and, when the occasional disaster struck, some institution like a religious organization advised us to accept it as an "act of God" or as a test of faith. Today, in a more secular age, we know considerably more about the nature of the world and its events, but that knowledge perversely increases our uncertainties!

Organizations, both profit and nonprofit, have a new need. It is an internal function that continually asks three questions. (1) When will something unexpected occur? (2) What can we do about it? (3) Can we survive? These questions and their answers constitute risk management, a discipline for living with the possibility that future events will materially affect us. Its scope will not be restricted to insurance, or even risk financing, but it will embrace holistically all forms of risk that affect the organization. It will look first at the ever-dynamic *global risks*, such as political fragmentation and consolidation, climate change, health improvements and pandemics, nuclear proliferation and controls, population changes, and the waxing and waning of religious fundamentalism. Most of these are seldom controllable by a single nation, much less a single organization, but management nonetheless needs to know and understand their implications. This risk management function will then focus on *organizational risks*, falling in four general areas:

- Financial/Market Risk: economic movements; capital availability; and foreign exchange, commodity, interest rate, credit and equity trading.
- Political/Regulatory Risk: state action; social change; war; terrorism; regulations
- Legal Liability Risk: contracts; torts; statutes; judicial decisions
- Operational Risk: technological change; information processing; criminal activity; personnel changes; direct and consequential effects on property.

These risks are controllable. They are susceptible to concrete assessment, control and financing. The "new" risk managers and the insurance industry will have to respond both strategically and tactically to *all* these risks if they are to preserve and improve their contributions to the organizations they serve.

I now move to seven suggestions for meeting the risk needs of organizations in the future. They apply to *all* managers, but especially to those who now practice insurance management and who wish to expand their responsibilities to a broader arena.

1. **A new language of risk** Risks are measured and assessed in many different ways. We need to develop a new composite language of risk, understandable to the layman, building on such tools as actuarial science, probabilistic and quantitative risk assessment, and qualitative techniques such as Delphi and scenario analysis (see Peter Schwartz and Dr. Vernon Grose). This new language, incorporating both quantitative and qualitative measures, should address the key elements of volatility (frequency and severity) and correlation (how one risk or risk response affects others). I see some progress in this area. Union Carbide has a composite risk analysis that reports major situations directly to the Board. Leading financial institutions such as J. P. Morgan and Bankers Trust can deliver to their chief executive officers a daily summary of the institutional risk situation for all financial positions. In the future this daily summary will encompass *all* risks, operational, legal, political as well as financial/market. Risk management will thus become part of the culture of management, just as suggested by England's Cadbury Committee and by standards organizations in Australia, New Zealand and Canada.
2. **Tailored financing tools** Risk financing for an organization will become a composite of internal and external funding, capital and operational. Internal tools will include use of reserves, captive insurers, and significantly higher insurance deductibles, both horizontal and vertical. External tools will include equity (through institutional and individual investors), credit (long and short term), hedges, swaps, options, futures, and, yes, even traditional insurance and reinsurance. The major focus will be on "synthetic insurance," although in time I believe that, in time, tax laws will change so that internal risk reserving will be tax deductible, even as catastrophe reserves will have similar treatment for insurers. The key here will be the recognition by many major organizations that they can, indeed, accept much higher levels of risk retention. Already British Petroleum has inaugurated a progressive program of *no* commercial insurance *over* $10 million. Other large corporations in North America have implemented retention plans of $50 to $100 million. The key will be to mix and match a variety of financing tools from various sources to fit the risk profile of an individual organization. They will define their own risks and design appropriate responses, rather than submit to the outmode annual "insurance auction."
3. **Tailored services** The next decade will see the continuation of the process of unbundling services, one that started fifteen years ago. Organizations seek

a combination of high quality risk assessment and risk control supports for internal skills. They want those best adapted to their unique blend of problems, not accepting all the services from a single vendor, simply for convenience. Services will be networked. Some insurance risk managers operate in this fashion today, paying for each service on a time and expense basis. The acceptance of combined services from a single firm, paid by commissions or premiums, is a thing of the past.

4. **Direct access to underwriters** Organizations will deal directly with those who actually underwrite risks. Given the new techniques of communications, including email, faxes and video conferencing, this direct contact will spell the end of the traditional role of intermediaries. They will, in turn, become consultants rather than commission-paid brokers. Again, this process has already started. Recently one progressive insurance risk manager called leading underwriters from around the world (insurers and reinsurers alike) to a meeting at his head office to introduce an innovative new financing plan. Most signed on immediately. In the future insurance risk managers will have direct access to global risk and loss databases or peer groups and service organizations.
5. **Reduction of non-essential costs** The biggest albatross weighing down the insurance industry is its overhead cost structure. A 1994 Towers Perrin survey of insurance CEOs ranked this the second most important strategic issue, so the problem is not unrecognized. The issue is what to do about it! Most insurance risk managers believe that an expense ratio closer to 5% should be the goal. That is not as impossible as it sounds, but it will take radical rethinking to achieve it. Many large group captive insurers now operate at 5% or less. The average expense ratio of a group of domestic United States medical malpractice captives (with more than five year's experience) is less than 15%. Obviously every facet of expense must be reviewed. Can insurers operate directly with insurance buyers, ranging from the largest, to small businesses, and to individuals? Will customer be willing to pay fees, not commissions, to those who advise them? Can underwriting be simplified? Can the overhead costs of state regulation be trashed in favor of national regulation? Will it be less expensive? Can other related insurer services be offered on a fee basis? The answers to these questions may determine the future of the industry.
6. **Long-term partnerships** Back in 1985, I first advanced the idea of risk sharing and long-term partnerships between insurers and buyers. It was hardly a new idea then, since this concept has been the underpinning of many reinsurance agreements over the past century. The elements of sound long-term arrangements will include a written agreement, approved by the boards of both institutions, of from five to ten years, plus mutual cancellation provisions limiting the opportunity to withdraw, ancillary services on a fee basis, direct payment of premiums, linkage of premiums to a rolling average of actual incurred and actuarially determined "incurred but not reported" losses, and, finally, provision

of large net line capacity from individual insurers equal to or greater than the retention of the insured. These new partnerships, arranged with fewer insurers, will clearly illustrate the truth of my contention that "there is no such thing as risk transfer; there is only risk sharing."

7. **Linkage with society** Risk management in the future will address not only the narrow needs of shareholders, employees and customers, but also the broader requirements of suppliers, regulators, the communities in which organizations operate, plus society as a whole. We can no longer put on blinders about the effects of our actions on the complete set of stakeholders for any organization. One positive benefit may come in meeting catastrophes. Coordination of risk assessment, control and financing efforts among private organizations, the private insurance sector, and governments (local, national and global) can create response mechanisms that will protect us all more effectively. In addition, a more proactive effort can, over time, re-establish the regulatory, judicial and legislative environment most conducive to economic growth and the strength of our respective institutions.

Many may not accept my original theses that both the insurance industry and the risk management discipline are failing in their current responsibilities, but there are enough signs of failure to warrant a fresh and critical look at both, and especially at how they interact with each other. It is time, I believe, to reconsider every aspect of insurance and risk management to determine how each will respond to the challenges of the future.

Remember Thomas Mendip's skeptical view of the moon a "circumambulating aphrodisiac," and be willing to apply an equally skeptical approach to your own work. And finally remember my two koan-like suggestions: "insurance is a pre-funded line of credit," and" there is no such thing as risk transfer; there is only risk sharing." If any of these ideas help move us toward a new appreciation of both insurance and risk, my work will have been successful.

Eleven years later, with little change visible, and with the insurance industry imploding under the attacks of regulators in several states, I expressed my continued frustration.

2005 Paper: Is Anyone Listening?

Four recent events challenge my credulity! Is it possible that no one is listening?

- Aon, in London, announced that, instead of accepting contingency commissions, previously and piously renounced, it will levy "fees" on insurers for the various "services" that it says it must continue to provide to them. These fees, strangely, appear to replace the lost commissions and perhaps reduce somewhat the $190 million the firm promised in restitution to clients.

- Marsh, in New York, demonstrating ultimate *chutzpah,* trumpeted these words in a full-page ad in *The New York Times*: "*We* ended the use of contingent compensation to avoid any perception of conflict of interest," and "*We* established an $850 million fund to compensate clients who placed insurance through Marsh in the United States." What is this "*We?"* It was the AG of New York who *forced* the brokerage firm to rescind contingent commissions and to establish a compensation fund! Here is Orwellian Newspeak at its worst!
- AIRMIC, an organization that purports to represent insurance buyers in UK, just announced the creation of a "partnership agreement" with three brokers and seven insurers under which this group will pay AIRMIC £400,000 a year to support "new research and services" (unspecified) in return for "improved contact with AIRMIC and its members." This is incredible in light of what has just been disclosed in the United States and in the UK!
- After continued disclosures of self-dealing, AIG "retires" its longtime CEO, Hank Greenburg, but he remains as chairman of several relatively obscure holding companies, one of which controls the compensation of most of the remaining senior executives.

We need a complete change in the traditional insurance business model. Half-measures, newspeak and business as usual cannot restore the trust and confidence that we've lost in the entire system.

Trust and confidence are the heart of our global financial system, but we've experienced nothing but disillusion! It's a continued plague in financial services—accountants seduced by consulting fees, stockbrokers touting the companies that reward them the most, mutual funds allowing timing trades, pension advisors looking the other way when employees plow their IRAs into company stock, pension actuaries allowing assumptions that permit under-funding, executive compensation consultants encouraging wildly inflated executive pay, and insurance "advisors" accepting payments from the vendors they were hired to select.

The Attorney General of New York found what many of us have known for more than thirty years—a commission system under which the seller pays the representative of the buyer is inherently flawed. Sooner or later it invites the sort of behavior chronicled over the past twelve months.

This problem is not new. I wrote about it in 1971: "Many of the national brokerage houses operate as both brokers and agents, depending on the circumstances. Under certain agreements, they have negotiated additional contingency commission arrangements in which they share with the insurance company the 'profit,' if any, accruing from a favorable loss ratio. If a broker represents himself as serving his client, *there is no moral or economic reason* for him to collect a contingency commission from an insurance company." Nothing has changed.

Insurance is a business riddled with conflicts of interest, anachronistic practices, archaic regulation (especially in the United States) and a chauvinistic self-view. How can you trust an advisory firm that takes almost all its income from the very insurers that it is charged with recommending to its clients, that invests directly or indirectly in insurers or reinsurers, that accepts commissions that are contingent on insurer desires or profits, that invests fiduciary funds (delaying client dollars sent to insurers) for its own account, and demands the right to place reinsurance for these same insurers?

This system is not illegal—it is simply unethical and irrational. In the law of the State of New York, Section 2101makes a broker the "legal representative" of the insured. But how can this be if the brokers receive all their remuneration from the seller?

The buyers know but they do not seem to care! In May 2004, the Risk & Insurance Management Society (RIMS) commented: "Our members appreciate what the broker is doing. They don't care where the payments are coming from as long as they are disclosed." RIMS didn't ask for "disclosure" until 1999 and even afterwards few buyers received any such notice. Buyers are as complicit as their insurers, brokers and regulators in accepting and perpetuating a system that was bound to lead to corruption.

Any income from other than a client corrupts a relationship that must be built on trust. How can a buyer be sure that a bid is not rigged, that fictitious "services" are not being offered, that its interests are not being subverted for greater income to the broker? How can an insurer believe that it is receiving honest information from a broker? How can directors of a public company be sure that their insurance buyer is not complicit in a fiddled system?

Disclosure is a band-aid, a half step toward reinstating trust. It is not enough! Responsibility for this mess rests with the brokers, the insurers *and* the buyers: they are all complicit!

What can we do? A few recommendations can begin to change the situation.

- Brokers should scrap immediately *all* commissions, both contingent and direct.
- Clients should pay brokers a mutually negotiated fee, based on published hourly rates. (Is this so hard? Accountants, advertising agencies, lawyers and consultants are all paid on this basis.) Fees are no guarantee against unethical behavior, but they reduce the potential.
- Buyers should negotiate directly with insurers, pay their premiums directly, and pay no premium until a *correct* and current policy contract is in hand.
- Buyers should make their claims directly to insurers and payments should go directly to the buyers.
- Buyers should push immediately for federal regulation of the insurance business in the United States and for more consistent global regulation.

Is anyone listening?

It seems that few paid any attention. So I tried again!

2007 Paper: Deaf Ears and No Voices

More than sixty-five years ago a prominent Philadelphia lawyer, in a speech to an insurance audience, cautioned the assembled underwriters, agents and brokers that their basic business model had a serious flaw: it was based on the payment of commissions as the primary incentive to sell policies. This lawyer noted that the commission system not only corrupted the objectivity of the sales staff but also encouraged "selling" rather than "counseling."

More than half a century later, we've made no progress whatsoever. The insurance industry remains mired in blatant conflicts of interest. Despite periodic disclosures of manipulation and skullduggery, the latest having been the investigations of Eliot Spitzer when he was Attorney General of New York State, the industry just does not want to hear about it. The disclosures fall on deaf ears. The industry either cannot or doesn't want to hear! And the saddest part of this long story is that its customers, for many reasons, have lost their voice: they seem congenitally unable to say a word about this woeful system, except "transparency," a feeble bleat as they are led to the slaughter once again. They have been so financially and intellectually co-opted by their insurers and agents (there is no such thing as a "broker," one who truly represents a client) that they have become mute.

The two most egregious conflicts of interest are the extra or "contingent" commissions that agents collect contrary to their clients' best interests (basic commissions are almost as bad!) and the growing investments of intermediaries in insurance companies.

The contingent commission situation is appalling. Mr. Spitzer first uncovers the fact that these commissions exist ("I'm shocked, shocked," as the Inspector said in *Casablanca*), and then finds that (unbelievable!) brokers actually direct their business to earn the highest commissions. He then extorts an agreement from several of the leading firms to refuse to accept contingent commissions in the future. What do they do? They begin negotiating with insurers for higher basic commissions and encourage these same insurers to offer a new "fixed compensation program based on prior years' performance!" What a lovely euphemism! No "contingent commissions" based on "profitability, volume, or desired class of business" but rather a "performance bonus." And all the while the sheep's chorus from the Risk & Insurance Management Society (RIMS) bleats only one word, "transparency." I think I now understand the meaning of "The Silence of the Lambs." The buyers don't want another system and few want to know what their "agents" really earn. The intermediaries involved in this manipulation give new depth to the oxymoron "honest broker." I suppose they think that, since Mr. Spitzer is now Governor of New York instead of simply its Attorney General, he will be involved in bigger issues.

The second piece of this travesty is equally disturbing. Earlier this year the press announced that Robert Clements, the founder of a new insurance brokerage firm, Integro, formed from the ashes of the Marsh-Aon-Willis-Gallagher mess, purportedly to bring fresh integrity to the business, has helped create and invest in a new Bermuda insurer, Ironshore Ltd. Wonderful: now we have one-stop shopping with an intermediary, supposed to select markets solely on their objective worth, directing a client's insurance to a company in which it has a major financial interest. You may not need a contingent commission when you receive a handsome dividend from the insurer every year!

I have yet to see one word of caution from the buyers' community. Perhaps their hands are so firmly wrapped around their ankles that they can't see what is going on (or they're seeing the past upside-down).

For those organizations that require some form of insurance for asset protection, their access to this confused market is so constricted by conflicts and misshapen regulations that *caveat emptor* is the only rational guide. If a buyer wants to pay an intermediary solely on a fee basis or go directly to an underwriter, he will find that forty-eight of the fifty US states do not permit buyers to negotiate commissions with their intermediaries. Some insurers file their rates with a commission that *must* be paid (as in workers' compensation). Insurers *force* you to go through an agent. In order to gain access to multiple insurers, a buyer may therefore have to work through many different agents and brokers, as all limited their placements. This was acknowledged by Dan H te, a senior officer in a Nashville, Tennessee-based firm, in a candid interview in *Leader's Edge Magazine,* the official publication of the Council of Insurance Agents and Brokers (January-February 2007), in which he said: ‘If you are an average broker—and don't care whether you are a national broker, regional broker or small mom and pop—they all have about four markets they use. They may have contracts for more, but they have four they routinely use. They will continue to use them because, if they don't, they are going to go broke trying to spread around the business too widely. You have to be efficient, and that means three, maybe four carriers.” This same executive then argued that concentrating business would help in claims problems. Oh? With a handsome profit contingent commission (or the new “performance bonus”), how interested will a “broker” be in presenting your large claim when it will kill next year's bonus? He is hopelessly conflicted.

What's the solution? It is the same as suggested more than fifty years ago. Change the regulation of insurers to federal instead of the archaic state system corrupted by the agency/commission system. Teach insurers to market directly. Adopt new technology to enhance direct access. Pay intermediaries on a fee basis, based on their professional time, so that they will be more likely to be objective.

What is the likelihood that these changes will be made? Less than five percent until buyers regain their voices and sellers begin to hear.

> So true is it that great institutions are undone as much by presumable guardians as by enemies.
>
> **Jacques Barzun, *From Dawn to Decadence,***
> **HarperCollins, New York 2000**

CHAPTER 8

Don't Step on the Tail of a Tigress!

James Thurber wrote often and glowingly about the eternal war between the sexes. In many, but not all, parts of this globe, women have not only achieved equality with men but they have also sometimes made it impossible to speak of possible disparities.

> Marriage has many virtues and one not often remarked upon by bachelors is that it helps to persuade a man that he is neither omniscient nor even infallible. A husband has but to utter a wish for it to be denied, countered, crossed, contradicted; or to hear the word *but,* followed by a pause, a very short pause in general, while the reasons that this wish should not be observed are marshaled—it is misconceived, contrary to his best interests, contrary to his real desires.
>
> **Patrick O'Brian, *The Nutmeg of Consolation,***
> **W. W. Norton & Co., New York 1991**

The Tigress: Is She Different?

I enter this debate with trepidation! As many readers know, even those at the far reaches of this globe, the President of Harvard University, Lawrence Summers, suggested, in a recent symposium that studied why mathematics and the sciences had relatively fewer women representatives than men, that perhaps, just perhaps, the problem might be attributed to some innate differences between the sexes. Oh my! The immediate outpouring of vitriol, including one woman academic who walked out on the President's speech, swamped all reasonable discourse and forced Mr. Summers to apologize and retract his words. A small portion of the faculty then voted no confidence in the President, and he ultimately resigned. Here again is an example of ideology, fixed political opinion, and years of fighting entrenched discrimination overwhelming any possibility of rational discussion.

As the initial tidal wave of feminine acrimony subsided, others stepped in. Some noted that it is the manifest responsibility of academic leaders to ask probing, difficult and often embarrassing questions. That's the essence of intellectual stimulus. Then others cited the differences that set males and females apart. Boys, *The Economist* wrote, are "four times more likely to be autistic than girls." A new medical study announced that taking an aspirin a day reduces the chance of heart attack for men but not women. Are women therefore less susceptible to heart attack? Only women can bear children, requiring time for this responsibility. So what's new? Women and men *are* different, but does that tell us anything about the unique capabilities of an individual woman or man? Is it a social (and potential legal) disaster if every profession, every discipline, every job is not precisely divided by the prevailing male/female ratio in the population?

The discipline of risk management offers some guidance. Too much of this current debate is based on possible negative outcomes, the potential inability of someone to command a skill or succeed in a job. Just as risk management shortchanges itself by addressing only negative results, so too does society but looking only at possible lack of capabilities.

I suggest, for once, we look at the positive side of the natural differences that exist in our species. Rather than deny them, or create artificial barriers to block people or incentives to spur them, why not look for the unique characteristics that make one sex or another better equipped for certain jobs.

Begin such an analysis with time, our finite resource. Rampant workaholism—the tendency to require and glorify the notorious eighty-hour week—contributes to the myth that some women can't hack it in the modern world, especially when they try and balance a career with childrearing. For success in law, consulting, the sciences, politics and many other careers, the prevailing mantra is "more time is better, and if you aren't willing to spend it, you're out!" By accepting this mantra, we've not only cut off access to a talented half of the population but we may, at the same time, have increased the risk of dogmatism and reduced the chances for insight and creativity.

Many years ago, Blaise Pascal was said to have written a long letter to a friend, apologizing that "if I had more time, my letter would have been shorter," implying that more time equals better output. Was Pascal wrong? I think so. More time devoted to a task does not *necessarily* mean that the quality of the output, the decision, the conclusion, is any better. Quality is determined less by the total hours then by how a mind grapples with a problem, its ability to create that "Eureka!" moment of insight. And herein lies the quality that women may bring to the table. Are women, innately, better managers of time, better producers of insight? Is it possible that, because they are biologically required to master many totally different tasks within a workday, they can apply less time to problems with better results? The current business jargon calls this "multi-tasking." Are women better at it?

My answer is based on empirical evidence gathered over forty years. I cite experience with one female associate, one spouse and three daughters. In the 1970s my consulting firm hired a female associate for administrative responsibilities. She had one child and became pregnant with a second. We gave her time off for the birth of a son, simply telling her to let us know when she felt comfortable returning to part-time or full-time work. After two months she asked to do work at home, following that with part-time work in the office, and then returning full-time, even though she often left the office at 4:30 p.m. for her home responsibilities. This was all flexible time, long before it was the norm and had a name, and for almost two years, she worked less than the conventional eight-hour day. My point: during all that time her productivity *exceeded* those who worked the usual hours. The presumed limitation of her femininity was well offset by her productivity. That experience was echoed by my spouse's work for a local architect. She drafted only six hours a day, and skipped lunch, so that she could manage a home for a husband and four children and also play with a ladies' tennis group three afternoons a week. When I asked him about this arrangement, most unusual thirty-five years ago in the United States, he told me that she produced in those six hours more than any other draftsman in his office produced in eight. Finally, I've watched, with growing admiration, three daughters raise nine grandchildren and still manage a variety of careers ranging from high-pressured executive in New York City and a university employee, to home-schooling.

While this admittedly modest sample could be part of a deductive fallacy, it does suggest that women, possibly, may manage time better. In some instances they can be *more* productive in less time. Their obstacle is our illusion that the Pascal principle can be taken to extremes. We spend too much raw time doing something and too little time thinking about what we should do, too little time managing that time, too little time cleansing our minds by doing something completely different.

There's a second aspect to how we use time. Several years ago I used the analogy of solving a crossword puzzle to show that one large block of time does not serve nearly so well as several small blocks, separated by different mental and physical pursuits. I proved it again one morning in March. As soon as I was stumped by a Friday *New York Times* puzzle, I stopped and spent several hours writing and doing chores. When I returned to the puzzle in the late afternoon, I managed to finish all but a quarter. Again, I tried different work, coming back to the crossword after dinner, at which time I completed it easily. Just over an hour, separated into three short segments, allowed me to do something that even three hours of concentrated time could not achieve. My point is that large blocs of time may be less productive than several shorter periods separated by totally different work, mental and physical.

I suggest that women, naturally designed and required to play many different roles, may not only be able to show greater productivity in less time, but also be more insightful. If my theses are correct, they tell us we should re-design the entire idea of "work" to take advantage of the difference. As Judith Shulevitz wrote in *The New York Times* (February 20, 2005), "until we change our bedrock assumptions about what the proper balance of work and life should be, women will always pay a price for interrupting their careers to have children." As it is today, we are mesmerized by "obsessive time-maximizers" (in the words of David Brooks) who engage themselves in a life-long "productivity marathon." Are we inadvertently punishing the more adaptable?

It was not so long ago that women were considered chattels. The Chinese bound women's feet to reduce mobility. The Abrahamic religions swathed them in cloth from head to toe (the habits of Christian nuns, the chadors and burkhas of Islam), customs that persist today. We still fight entrenched superstition and discrimination. But, if we try and look for the innate differences that make women *better* equipped to contribute to society, then we may avoid the unnecessary uproar that followed an academic's suggestion that these differences exist.

Time is a finite asset. More of it does not necessarily mean a better outcome. Managing time more intelligently will help all of us, and women may just be better managers of time. And, who knows, men might be able to learn from them.

Something truly ridiculous often restores balance.

Sense of the Ridiculous

Several months ago I watched a DVD of Charles Dickens' *Nicholas Nickleby,* an engaging, amusing rendition of a novel I read forty years ago. In it, Nathan Lane and Dame Edna Everidge, two incomparable character actors ("she" is a he) played the parts of two of the traveling actors' troupe, emphasizing much of the ridiculousness of the entire story. It was almost Voltaire. It caught me at a moment when I was taking this idea of risk management a bit too seriously!

It is time to reinforce the thought that much of what we do is basically ridiculous. Isn't it ridiculous to think that we can tame uncertainty? In an earlier stage in human development, we adopted a faith that some system of gods or quantitative analyses would answer all questions. We've learned better. It's time to sustain our sense of doubt and curiosity—and optimism—so that our efforts in risk analysis and risk response carry a proper weight within organizations.

My dictionary defines "ridiculous" as "laughable; absurd; silly; preposterous," but the ridiculous can actually be profound, witness the thought processes stimulated by a Zen koan ("what is the sound of one hand clapping?" or "The goose is in the bottle: how does it get out? There: it's out!"). Let's reconsider risk management as the Theatre of the Absurd!

> The very essence of romance is uncertainty.
>
> **Oscar Wilde, *The Importance of Being Ernest***

CHAPTER 9

The Nature of Risk and Fear

> And it surely is naïve to define discontinuity as anomaly instead of normality.
>
> **Peter L. Bernstein, "The New Religion of Risk Management,"**
> ***Harvard Business Review,* March-April 1996**

As I noted in the first chapter of this book, the word "risk" poses semantic difficulties for many of us, creating those fantods of the title. Some see it solely as a "bad event. Others see a more complex mixture of potentially favorable and unfavorable outcomes. Still others treat "risk" as volatility or as a physical entity. Here are a few essays on this conundrum.

Fear and the Future

For some time now I've expressed my worry about risk management becoming overly focused on unexpected downside events. I've argued that this creates an instinctive risk aversion that undermines our faith in a better future, a faith that for more than two centuries now has been the driving cultural and economic force in the United States.

Three recent events illustrate the difficulty of dealing with the present when we lose faith in the future and when raw fear dominates economic and political discussion. In France the President and Prime Minister supported a modest easing of antiquated and uneconomic employment practices as a start toward engaging that country with the realities of globalization. Almost immediately the fear of losing secure jobs stimulated the unions and, unbelievably, students into mass protests and strikes. Government backed down to fear, rewarding the forces of reaction, and France continues to lose ground to global competitors. At the same time, thousands of miles to the west, in Washington, the Congress of the United States grappled with the growing political backlash on the immigration issue. Our porous southern border has drawn over eleven million immigrants, many illegal, into this country from Mexico, Central and South America, for the obvious economic opportunities. A sensible answer to the problem is increasing border security, encouraging those already here to become legal citizens, and, simultaneously helping these nations to improve their economic conditions so that their citizens will no longer be inkling to migrate. As in France, the public raw fear of the future drives the Congressional response: the desire to return to some "better" imagined past, the famous *status quo ex post ante*. We are now considering the construction of a southern "wall." Neither the Great Wall of China nor the Berlin Wall protected those inside from the influx of people and ideas, and the wall under construction in Israel will probably fail too. A wall of fear never works!

Finally, in Detroit, General Motors' employees face another kind of present/future decision. Tilting on the edge of bankruptcy, the company is trying to reduce payroll and health costs by "buying out" over 100,000 workers. Their dilemma: should they opt to keep their jobs and current health benefits in the hope that both relatively handsome rewards will continue, or take the buyout (as much as $140,000 for employees with ten years on the job) and try to find another job and health benefits? Financial analysts, doing risk assessments, suggest that opting for the buyout is a better course, but this requires that elusive belief in the "future." GM is waiting for their decisions.

If we cannot see a better future and are willing to invest in it, then we will end up worshipping the present and past. The French students and their union leaders, the Neanderthals in Congress and GM employees could learn something from Henri-Georges Clouzot's 1953 film, *Wages of Fear*. In this movie, which I first saw in New York City in 1955 and religiously re-screen once a year, Yves Montand plays the part of Mario, a penniless drifter in a small Central American village dominated by a US oil company. He and his friends borrow money, avoid work and complain about their condition, hoping that someone else will pay for their repatriation to Europe. When an inland well of the oil company blows out, its manager, unwilling to risk the lives of his regular employees, offers a large financial reward if four of these drifters will agree to drive two trucks loaded with nitro-glycerin from the town to the well site, on over 100 miles of rutted and washboard dirt roads, with rock slides, switchbacks and rotting bridges. "I know what risk is!" claims Mario. It is a combination of fear and exhilaration, fear of the high probability of instant death balanced by an instant ticket home to Europe. All four men accept this "risk" and start on their journey to the well. Their fear of the future is eclipsed by their anticipation of reward. For them fear is their stimulus. And so the two trucks, sirens screaming, start off at two miles an hour. For the end of the story, see this film!

We cannot allow fear to destroy our faith in the future, but the current focus of risk management is doing just this. Intelligent risk taking, not risk avoidance, is the habit to encourage. David Rejeski and Robert Olson addressed this point with clarity in their article, "Has Futurism Failed?" in the Winter 2006 issue of *Wilson Quarterly.* The authors trace the "futures" movement, a means of describing plausible alternative futures, from its start in the early 1950s to the present. Today, "complexity theory" suggests an improved means of considering what may happen. They write: "While it dampens hopes that prediction will ever achieve a high degree of accuracy, complexity theory points to better approaches in dealing with surprises, disruption, and uncertainty. We must both prepare for the unexpected, in part by constantly revising our 'situational' awareness of the present, and work toward creating the kinds of long-term outcomes we want by crafting well-considered images of the future." These "images" or scenarios allow us the chance to "dare," an "indispensable quality in a nation of optimists", balanced by the "useful tonic" of "cautionary understanding." That imagined "better" future continues to be our driving force: ". . . people who embark on generational journeys are the realistic ones, because they are the ones who see all the possibilities the future contains." See also David Brooks, in "The Past Meets the Future," in *The New York Times,* April 14, 2006.

A problem coupled with fear of the future is the increasing new faith in numbers. Over the past 400 years we've developed new ideas and tools that enable us to convert some uncertainty into measurable "risk." Much of this development is based on mathematics. They allow us to approach the future with greater confidence, allowing us to believe we can actually modify what will come. Risk management, in this sense, is the successor to the old superstition we are guided only by fate. When we knew no better, we believed that various gods and goddesses foreordained what would occur. A hurricane, tornado, earthquake, eclipse, or flood was interpreted as the act of some "divine" creature, whose whims were interpreted by an oracle, imam or priest. Rational knowledge replaced these myths and superstitions. Today, we collect history and information into databases manipulated by econometric models whose "forecasts" and mathematical precision are received with almost the same awe, admiration and gullibility as the pronouncements of earlier soothsayers. We appear to be so intent on reducing volatility and uncertainty that we "replace old superstitions with a new faith in numbers." Over a decade ago, Peter Bernstein warned us of this inclination in his perceptive article in the March-April 1996 issue of the *Harvard Business Review,* "The New Religion of Risk Management." "We must consider the possibility that the whole process of breaking free from the Fates has turned us into slaves of a new kind of religion, a creed that is just as implacable, confining, and arbitrary as the old." Our new tools indeed permit us to take more risk more responsibly, but we can never trash doubt, curiosity and judgment. Peter warned against the "arrogance of quantifying the unquantifiable," "the hubris that we can put reliable and stable numbers on the impact of a politician's power, on the probability of a takeover boom, on the return on the stock market over the next 2, 20, or 50 years, or on the subjective factors like utility and risk aversion."

Are we actually regressing into an almost religious fear of adverse outcomes, with no view of the possible positive changes that may improve our world, and, at the same time, placing an almost religious faith in numbers? The "bitch-goddess quantification" (the descriptive words of the historian Thomas Jefferson Wertenbaker) may become as persuasive as crystal balls, tea leaves, "miracles" and stirring the excrement of bulls.

I redefined "risk" in the opening chapter. Here is a further set of variations on that theme.

What Exactly *is* Risk?

For some years now, I've been conducting a personal odyssey trying to bring both benefit and harm into our definition of the word "risk." In late December 2005, John Adams, the erudite author of *Risk* (1995) and professor at University College London, sent me for comment a draft of an article for the *Financial Times*. I took this opportunity to criticize his implication that risk involves only possible downside results. He in turn replied that I was, well, out of touch with the world!

"None of the dictionaries I have consulted," he wrote, "would agree that 'risk encompasses BOTH favorable and unfavorable outcomes'. In terms of my risk thermostat model, the word embraces only the bottom loop. Certainly risks are taken in pursuit of rewards, but to speak, for example, of 'taking the risk of making a lot of money' (as distinct from losing it), challenges not only most dictionary definitions but, more importantly, common parlance."

John Adams may well be right, but, like Cervantes' hero, I continue to try and overturn what appears to be the consensus definition of the word that defines our discipline. It may be a fruitless effort but I continue, undiminished and undeterred. If only I had a loyal Sancho Panza at my side!

Like John Adams, I scanned my dictionaries at home, plus several on the web. All emphasize the negative characteristic of the word as a noun: the possibility of suffering harm. Yet several counter with an option from the financial world: the variability of returns from an investment, which, in turns *implies both* favorable and unfavorable results beyond what is expected. This alternate definition does not appear in earlier editions (such as the 1944 Second Edition of Webster's New International), so perhaps it is indicative of a slow but important shift in our understanding of the word. Roget's Thesaurus (1959) suggests synonyms such as chance, gamble and dare for the verb. Don't these words show the possibility of plus and minus outcomes?

I even resorted to the famous Canadian Oxford Dictionary in its 1998 edition, given Dr. Adam's esteemed Ontario heritage. Its first two definitions use the standard view of harm and danger, but its third I found nowhere else: to "risk" is "to venture on," with a profound indication that we make decisions, we move on, taking chances for good *and* ill. Is this unique among the denizens of the Great White North? In 1998 I excerpted some comments from another sagacious Canadian, Douglas Barlow, who once wrote to me, "I see all management as risk management. It is an expression of an instinctive and constant drive for defense of an organism against the risks that are a part of the uncertainty of existence." He supported my working definition of risk management as "a discipline for dealing with uncertainty" and added that it is a "disciplined response to risks, expressive of an innate pro-life drive. "I see," Barlow continued, "the rewards-harm gamut as a continuum in which the categorization of the figure concerned, as 'reward' or 'harm,' is determined by its measurement from the place at which you choose the put the datum or zero point."

All this reinforces my belief that risk is a coherent measure of the possibility of an outcome different from the one expected. That's why I continue to admire Dr. Adams' own definition (from *Risk,* 1995): "a cultural construct that illuminates a world of plural rationalities." In a world that is forever uncertain, our ability to transform a small portion of the unknown into risk is indeed illuminating: it sheds light where there was none before. And those "plural rationalities" must either or both beneficial or harmful, depending on circumstances.

So I searched further, this time in John Bartlett's *Familiar Quotations,* 15th Edition, 1980, to see how others use the word.

In every quote I found some form of *implied* reward in the use of the word along with an explicit potential for harm. It is this unstated opposite that creates the tension and dynamic that we encounter with risk. It creates the joy of deciding! General George S. Patton said it best in 1944 to his grandson, then a cadet at the United States Military Academy at West Point: "Take calculated risks. That is quite different from being rash." We accept the possibility of harms in return for possible benefits that outweigh them: this is the calculation inherent in every decision that we make as individuals or organizations. To focus solely on possible downside results cheats us. It is only half of Patton's calculation.

Two of the great American philosophers of the 19th century had similar observations. James Russell Lowell wrote:

> And I honor the man who is willing to sink
> Half his present repute for the freedom to think,
> And, when he has thought, be his cause strong or weak,
> Will risk t'other half for the freedom to speak.
> (From *A Fable for Critics,* 1848)

And here is William James: "It is only by risking our persons from one hour to another that we live at all." (From *The Will to Believe,* 1897)

So despite the overwhelming conventional usage of the word to connote harmful outcomes, supported by those who write our dictionaries, I continue to struggle to plant the idea that every decision involves the possibilities of *both* favorable *and* unfavorable outcomes. If we simply accept common parlance and our learned lexicographers, we are apt to miss the essence of life!

- - - - - - - - - - - -

I shared these ideas with the good Dr. Adams. He is unconvinced!

His reply: "I hereby offer my services as your Sancho Panza. I read Don Quixote at university a million years ago—but it made a lasting impression. From memory Don Q was idealistic, but mad and deluded. Sancho struggled to make him see reality. Your version of risk is Dulcinea—a perfect, idealized, concept that no one else can see. I acknowledge that every decision involves the possibilities of favorable and unfavorable outcomes, but in common parlance we risk adverse outcomes in pursuit of favourable ones; we do not risk favourable outcomes. I think that Sancho would advise that to accept the common parlance version of risk is not to miss the essence of life, but to make one's contribution to discussions of this essence intelligible to a much wider audience. Don Q, after all was a failure. *Quixotic*, according to my on-line lexicographer, means 'foolishly impractical, especially in the pursuit of ideals.'"

My response to John Adams was that, if the word "risk" creates so much difficulty and leads us often in the wrong direction, perhaps we should scrap it. Should we replace it with "uncertainty" making it "uncertainty management," or a discipline for dealing with all contingencies?

Or perhaps my incessant musings on this subject should be treated as the trailings of Rocinante?

More variations of this theme

Risk, Plus and Minus

Many years ago, before I first retired (1993), I believed and wrote that risk management is "a discipline for living with the possibility that future events may cause harm." One day, while I was lecturing to a seminar at the University of St. Gallen, in Switzerland, a graduate student questioned this definition, arguing that outcomes could be *more* as well as *less* favorable than expected. That was my epiphany: I changed my mind and definition to incorporate the possibility of both benefit and harm. I mention this because, last month, I found a website paper in which I was quoted using that out-dated phraseology. I corrected the author and offer three recent examples to support my contention.

The first involves an unexpected outcome threatening an entire industry. The large, wire-dependent telephone companies face the collapse of their residential telephone income as their customers begin to move toward Internet telephone service from such upstarts as Vonage and Skype. This could easily become a stampede. It is the result of technological innovation and the continuing expansion of computer use by individuals. Did the risk officers at Verizon, Quest, and the other ex-Bell companies raise this strategic risk some years ago, when the idea first surfaced? As this downside risk explodes now, how do they respond? And aren't there some unseen opportunities? One failure to anticipate an unexpected development does not mean that the risk management process is worthless. It does mean that it should explore possible advantageous options, as well as take a long-view on future risks.

The second concerns an unexpected event that looked first to be favorable, but later, on further thought and experience, raised downside possibilities. In 2003, Joan Kroc, the wife of the founder of McDonald's, died and left the Salvation Army $1.5 *billion* to build 30 to 40 athletic and recreation centers in low-income neighborhoods around the United States. On the surface, such a bequest is an incredible plus. At the time, however, I questioned if there might be some downside repercussions, such as regular donors reducing or eliminating their annual contributions in light of the windfall. Others, within the Salvation Army, wondered if the bequest might alter the basic mission of the organization:

housing for the elderly, help for families in difficulty, disaster relief, and summer camps. And could the public perception of the Army change? This is an important role for risk management: to consider the possible downside repercussions from an unexpectedly favorable turn of events, as well as looking for silver linings in disasters. This is why the definition of "risk" must encompass both the good and the bad.

The third example is finding that silver lining. The U. S. Postal Service is experiencing a drop in first-class mail income, more than 1% from 2004 to 2005, in part a result of the dramatic increase in email correspondence. I can account for some of this. In 2000-2001 I mailed copies of and renewal notices for *Risk Management Reports* to my subscribers around the world. In April 2001 we converted to electronic delivery of both and the result was a continuing 80% reduction in postal expenses. The Postal Service saw this trend and, using risk management, I trust, has responded in an innovative fashion. As it recognized the inexorable shift to electronic mail, it also altered its strategy to take advantage of the Internet. As eBay exploded in growth, the USPS has become a major sponsor of this Internet auction house, offering its shipping services to eBay customers. According to news reports, its package shipping income increased 2.8% last year, as it stimulated it shipping income from such Internet companies as eBay, Amazon and Netflix.

These three examples illustrate the importance of risk management improving the flexibility and resilience or organizations facing unexpected outcomes. In our rapidly changing world, continuing risk assessments and scenario analyses are essential elements of sound risk management.

Three fantods on the risk issue

Why, Oh Why?

I'm an advocate of difficult questions, some unanswerable. They are similar to the weekly crossword puzzles that I attack in *The New York Times.* On Monday and Tuesday I do them in ink, with little effort. By Wednesday, however, I switch to a pencil with an eraser, often used. By Friday, I ask for help from my spouse, and on Saturday I generally give up. Here are a few of my "Saturday" questions.

Why, oh why, is it that so many risk management advocates refuse to acknowledge that unexpected events can be beneficial as well as harmful? Is it true that purveyors of "FUD" (fear, uncertainty and death) have more to gain from their ominous prognostications than from informing us that good things also are possible? Are there now ingrown industries (the insurance industry seems to be one of them) that spread fear and trepidation as their stock in trade? Some politicians tell us to elect them on the basis of all the bad things that could happen if they are not in power. Some gloom-meisters tell us that we will have to dispense with many of our hard-earned civil liberties if we are to defeat the monsters of terrorism. While I acknowledge that alarm gains attention, I have more optimism than pessimism.

Why, oh why, do we make the simple seem so complex? For many years I've tried, with an increasing sense of futility, to read the abstruse papers of academia, replete with embedded footnotes, passive sentences and multi-syllabic words. Just try one year of *Risk Management—An International Journal* or *Risk Analysis,* the quarterly of the Society for Risk Analysis, and you'll see what I mean. I do read the abstracts, but most of the articles that follow are academic gibberish. Are they even understandable to their fellow academics? And then delve into the machinations of the quants. These authors assume that every reader is an advanced mathematician. Can't some of these whizzes skip a beat and write coherent English? What ever happened to Strunk and White?

Why, oh why, do we so easily and quickly mis-estimate risk? We misconstrue the importance of context and chance, trying to create cause from correlation, when there is no connection. Why do we "extrapolate big conclusions from small samples, something that behavioral economists call the 'law of small numbers'"? (See James Surowiecki, in *The New Yorker,* July 31, 2006, who repeated many of our logical mathematical failures noted in John Allen Paulos' earlier excellent book, *Innumeracy.*) Surowiecki concluded: "Because we underestimate how much variation can be caused simply by luck, we see patterns where none exist."

And, finally, why is it that, as I grow older, I grow more cantankerous?

Why is it that we are so mesmerized of predictions of gloom and doom?

The Crippling Effects of Fear

Franklin D. Roosevelt famously addressed a nation in the throes of the Great Depression when he took office in 1933: "We have nothing to fear but fear itself." It was the first step in bringing the United States out of economic chaos. But today, I see many signs repeating that crippling fear of seventy years ago. Are we too easily frightened, too ready to see potential discouraging downside events, too anxious about the future to grasp the opportunities that lie ahead? We are starting to play defensive ball, which, as almost all sports analysts will tell you, is how to lose the game.

Three examples illustrate this malaise. The first happened at a May quarterly meeting for investors run by two stockbroker friends. As a preface to their remarks about the predicted trends in the markets over the next three months, they posted a list of their "fears." Here they are, and most will acknowledge that they are real and important:

- — Slowing economic growth in the United States
- — Weakening US dollar
- — Rising interest rates
- — Inflation, especially in the United States
- — Declining consumer confidence
- — The international housing bubble
- — Energy prices
- — Geopolitical uncertainty
- — The deficit in the United States

— Global economic conditions
— Increasing protectionism in Europe and the United States
— Terrorism

I don't deny that these are valid concerns, but a realistic analysis of each "fear" shows positive counterparts! This is exactly what I have been preaching for so many years: an unexpected event has both positive and negative consequences; we cripple our creativity if we look only at the downsides.

Consider these options:

— Slowing economic growth in the United States: but this growth may be steadier and more predictable, thus enhancing investment.
— Weakening US dollar: but this will encourage others to buy goods and services from the United States.
— Rising interest rates: this will attract more external investors to US securities.
— Inflation, especially in the United States: economists tell us that modest inflation is desirable; it has been low for some years.
— Declining consumer confidence: but this may stimulate a needed increase in personal savings.
— The international housing bubble: bubbles need to be deflated, even burst, thus enhancing future economic growth.
— Energy prices: high prices will stimulate a more serious search for alternative energy sources, helping the climate, political dependencies, costs, etc.
— Geopolitical uncertainty: geopolitics is always uncertain! What's new?
— The deficit in the United States: our growing awareness means that we will do something serious about the deficit.
— Global economic conditions: as with geopolitics, these are *always* volatile.
— Increasing protectionism in Europe and the United States: a minor backward step in the long march toward freer global trade.
— Terrorism: the actual frequency of terrorist events is sharply reduced from the years 1970-1990: global attention is producing results!

I do not propose a Pollyannaish response to these fears. I do suggest that a more balanced view of the potential unexpected events of the future will allow us both to take advantage of new opportunities and to reduce the effects of negative events. This is the goal of risk management: to enhance our native resiliency.

The second illustration was also local. Periodically the Defense Department in the United States is asked to review its holdings of military bases and similar property in line with its changing mission. This inevitably leads to the shutdown of some facilities, many of which have been economic mainstays to their communities. Even though the process is insulated against political pressures, it creates the usual outcry when the periodic shutdown list is published. This spring (2006) the submarine base in Groton, Connecticut, close to where I live, was on the list. The first headline was "Region Shocked, Angered by

Possibility of Shutdown," with every politician screaming bloody murder. Should we have been surprised? Hardly, as this base appeared on a prior shutdown list and as submarines now play a reduced role in current military plans. Every commentator described in horrific terms the economic pain the region might experience and argued that we should be spared (even as these same politicians demand that government cut its expenditures to reduce the deficit!) In other words, cut costs, but not in my backyard! It took almost a month before some saner observers noted that the property in question was prime waterside real estate, always in demand, and that some creative and imaginative thinking might just produce new businesses that would more than replace the lost sub base income to the region. In other words, the proposed shutdown could be an opportunity for all of us! Here again the driving force of fear obscured the other side of the equation. Yes, it is a very human reaction but good risk management requires immediate consideration of the balance.

My third illustration is the negative reaction to the Sarbanes-Oxley law in the United States (and comparable regulations in other countries). Compliance will cost considerable money and the regulatory burden will be heaviest on the smaller public firms. I've already noted the degree to which the accounting profession, both internal audit and external accounting, has focused on compliance almost to the exclusion of any balanced view of risk management. All this discourages managers from taking any risks. Yes, there will be benefits, including a slow but sure re-establishment of trust in public companies and the figures that they publish, but at what cost? If these laws and regulations, and our reaction to them, dampen risk taking and create new "defensive management," we are likely to become a horde of lemmings, reluctant to do anything different or "risky" for fear of legal or public opinion retribution.

The solution to these three examples is to swim against the prevailing tide of disillusionment and fear. Be contrary! When considering an action decision, list both favorable and unfavorable unexpected outcomes. A balanced analysis of risk is our proper course. But, while being contrary, don't jump off the cliff just because all the lemmings are running away from it!

> Innovation is the driving force behind value creation and competitive advantage, but you can't innovate and grow unless you are willing to take risks. Yet in the current regulatory and tort environment, companies are more focused on risk reduction than ever before. They're practicing defensive management by reducing R & D and other investments that Wall Street might punish for being too focused on the long-term or that could lead to regulatory challenges or litigation.
>
> **Deborah Wince-Smith, "Innovate at Your Own Risk,"**
> ***Harvard Business Review,* May 2005**

More commentary on the nature of uncertainty

The Uncertainty Principle

Listening to the presentations at many enterprise risk management conferences, I am struck by how often the projected risk outcomes, generally unfavorable, are considered fixed and defined by speakers. Does it make sense to accept variability in likelihood and the range of consequences but accept specific results as fixed in stone?

Every decision creates new possibilities of unexpected events or situations, with various possibilities of occurrence and outcomes. Yet when an event occurs, we construe their outcomes as fixed and inevitable. This disregards the rule of constant change: our own responses and those of others continually alter results. Therefore we can never analyze risks independently of one another, in a vacuum. Doing so creates further surprise.

Risks, the chances of unexpected outcomes, are part of a pulsing portfolio, much like a tub of worms. Some will catch fish; others will stink up the place. Each affects the others in a constantly changing fashion, and that is why we learn to assess risks as an organizational portfolio, rather than in the old-fashioned and outmoded individual way. At the same time other fishermen with other tubs of worms are operating, changing the scene for catches and foul odors for each other. Assuming today's risk analysis tells us something "certain" about the future is as foolish as expecting today's weather forecast to guarantee next week's weather. The inputs are constantly changing and so too are the outcomes. When an unexpected event or situation occurs, others respond, altering the climate. Measuring the quantitative effect of these responses is almost impossible, although sophisticated scenario analyses might suggest some. Organizational resilience becomes the more important goal. Consider the tub of worms!

A second factor in the indeterminacy of risk is the change in individual and organization perceptions after unusual events. It is impossible to pin down an outcome in time or space, akin to Werner Heisenberg's Uncertainty Principle in quantum mechanics. While I'm not as knowledgeable in physics as my more learned Copy Editor, I see similarities that apply to risk management. Risks remain constantly moving targets, always uncertain. Risk analysis is a temporary and incomplete means of aiding our decision process. It provides only a momentary glimpse of reality and then it is gone.

For example, take an astronaut's decision to fly to the moon. An initial risk assessment shows an upside potential for acclamation, fame and perhaps financial reward. The downside potential is death. That assessment, however, must go further to treat perception: death, a downside, may result in an upside, fame, (see Gus Grissom, for example). If fame is the primary goal, the decision to fly is automatic.

Perception can also alter one's reaction to an outcome. A young Islamist fanatic views death differently from a secularist of the same age. The fanatic sees a martyr's death as an opportunity to enter a paradise with a host of "virgins." The secularist sees only finality and the cessation of opportunity.

Consider two other intriguing aspects of risk. First, most of us prefer to avoid situations that pose extreme danger of bodily harm. Some, however, seek these "challenges" as to heighten their experience, similar to a drug-induced "high." In the May 22, 2006 issue of *The New Yorker* Anthony Lane wrote: "The obvious answer is that life can sometimes acquire a wilder flavor and a stronger concentration as the prospect of losing it draws near." Some organizations experience the same feeling when managers "bet the farm" on a single course of action. Both gamblers and stock market traders report this sense of heightened awareness. Second, science tells us the human body, in high pain, is capable of controlling its pain-modulating system, completely blocking out any sensation. Could organizations possibly do the same thing?

So we acknowledge our risks affect one another, systemically, because they are part of an organization's total portfolio, our own responses and those of others affect outcomes in a continuing fashion, and, most importantly, individual and group perceptions color outcomes as much as any arbitrary "reality." This suggests strongly that we must view our attempts at risk analysis more subjectively.

Often I fear there is no common language of risk. We are losing our ability to communicate as new parochial languages dominate discussion.

Financial Risk Management

While teaching sailing every summer to both juniors and adults, I first caution that they are about to learn a new language. It may sound like English to their ears, but, in reality, it is a composite of unfamiliar words created over the centuries by sea adventurers. Words such as "port" and "starboard" that mean left and right, "forward" and "aft," "head," "tack" and "clew" for the three sharp angles of any sail, and commands such as "bear off" and "head up," barked at a volume uncommon ashore, create an initial confusion that sometimes sends them back to land, never to set foot on a boat again. You go "below" or "aloft," cook in the "galley" and roost on the "head." And duct tape holds everything together!

I know how they feel. I've been reading, writing and speaking about "risk management" for more than 45 years, but I still find some aspects of our discipline almost incomprehensible. The arcane language of the public policy risk analysts, couched in mathematical formulae, appears every month in the journal of the Society for Risk Analysis, *Risk Analysis*, where I'm reduced to reading the abstracts for any usable information. I also groan at the complexity of the math used by financial risk managers at their annual GARP and PRMIA meetings, where I try to decipher all those Greek symbols and such tongue-tumbling conundrums such as "heteroscedasticity," "eigenvalues," and "cholesky decomposition."

I'm sure that this new language is as important to those who learn and use it as the language of sailing is to sailors. It's that, my advanced age, I have difficulty learning it. Early this summer, these thoughts were stimulated by the arrival of two new books. The first, the *Professional Risk Managers' Handbook,* purports to be the "ultimate" in information on financial risk. Given its size alone, it may be. It is a daunting three volumes and 1,300 pages. Each volume requires a sturdy book-rest for reading: don't try these in bed or, in the morning, your spouse may find you crushed to death. In contrast, the second is a mere 214 pages, is a jewel of clear prose and challenging thoughts. In 2004, *The Economist* published *Dealing With Financial Risk,* by David Shirreff. I read the second and scanned the first but both improved my financial risk management language skills.

Shirreff's book is a delight. Avoiding academic or mathematical jargon, it traces a cogent history of recent problems and provides a solid introduction to this particular sub-discipline. He correctly warns against the avalanche of "noise" that impairs our ability to understand current events ("like Pavlov's dogs, we are being conditioned to salivate or recoil as massed ranks of financial news sources pump out their messages"), against the "delusion" that financial models can outsmart the market over time, and against the hubris that dealing with financial risk is anything but a game. Shirreff begins with a history of the growth of modern financial markets, in which the "unbundling" of many financial instruments creates a growing need to know the counterparty. He then describes market theory (at last I begin to understand some of these ideas!), derivatives, and the magic (and risks) of leverage. He dissects the rise of sophisticated financial models that purport to predict the future, allegedly substituting certainty for uncertainty. These are the very models that led to the LTCM fiasco. "Beware," he says, "the outer wings of the bell curve" and the convoluted monetary incentives that drive traders to even riskier behavior. The theme of this book is that our "attempts to predict and master what is in effect (our) own collective behaviour have always and will constantly fall short of reality." We can collect more data. We can learn more about risk. We can modify risk. But we can never know or control it. His analysis of the development of the Basel accords shows that their efforts in understanding and managing global "systemic" risk may actually increase it, a warning made earlier by Avinash Persaud in his lectures in London. The more the larger banks worldwide tend to follow the same processes, for fear of being out of line, the more likely is a systemic breakdown. Shirreff argues for more focus on liquidity than on bank capital, for greater availability of funding allowing the system to absorb and manage the failure of one or more institutions, and for longer time horizons for risk measurement (ten years instead of one month). He predicts financial risk managers and their regulators "will eventually come to support *role-playing* and *simulation* (my italics) as a vital additional tool for keeping financial institutions and their supervisors up to the mark." I've always believed that approaches as scenario analysis are more effective that any simulations based on past data.

His final words should be committed to memory: "Financial risk management means a healthy distrust of experts—flat-earthers who know exactly what forces are driving the world economy, GDP figures, bond prices and world capital flows. Nothing is so certain. No rule works quite so well as the one which says that what goes up must come down."

At the end of the book, Shirreff includes a worthwhile glossary of financial terms, plus a brief list of recommended reading, one that includes Peter Bernstein and Nassim Taleb.

The Professional Risk Managers' Handbook is the physical antithesis of Shirreff, yet, together with his book as an introduction, it is a valuable reference resource. Edited by Carol Alexander and Elizabeth Sheedy, its three volumes are the official handbooks for the PRM certification examinations offered by the Professional Risk Manager's International Association (for more information on both the book and the certification, contact PRMIA at *www.prmia.org*).

As David Koenig, the Executive Director of PRMIA explains in his introduction, "financial risk management is not about avoiding risk. Rather, it is about understanding and communicating risk, so that risk can be taken more confidently and in a better way." The first (and heaviest) volume dissects financial theory, financial instruments and markets and leads off with a fascinating paper on "Risk and Risk Aversion," by Jacques Pézier, of the University of Reading, UK, who draws heavily on the prospect theory work of Kahneman and Tversky. In the continuing attempt to balance the potentials of reward and harm, human and organizational aversion to harm takes precedence, a natural tendency against which risk managers must fight. The second volume describes the mathematical foundations of risk measurement, leading to the nature of volatility and the use (and misuse) of VaR. Despite the overwhelming dominance of quantitative techniques in this volume, one of the editors, Carol Alexander, cautions, "quantification will never be a substitute for good risk management." The third and final volume addresses the three major risk arenas, market, credit and operational. It is a useful library of information on financial risk

While these two new publications improve my financial risk language skills, I doubt that I will ever be as proficient with them as I am with the words of sailing, which I've studied for more than sixty years.

> The standards that crept in during the 1990s condoned rapacity on behalf of bankers and their institutions and rewarded it, whereas scruples about the client's best interests were seen as squeamish and weak . . . . The culture of grabbing what you could get away with grew by leaps and bounds during the stockmarket boom years of 1986 to 2000.
>
> **David Shirreff, *Dealing With Financial Risk*,**
> **The Economist/Profile Books Ltd., London 2004**

CHAPTER 10

Ideas and Global Risks

Our risk understanding requires big ideas, big stories, and a global view. Here are four essays embodying this thought.

> In the end, to have an effect on the world, the mathematical risk models need to be translated into stories. However, that is troublesome because many risk managers and many of those who listen have never heard such stories before. We are all in new territory.
>
> **David Ingram, "Risky Stories," *Risk Management*, Society of Actuaries, November 2004**

Peter Bernstein's Big Ideas

My favorite guru, the octogenarian Peter Bernstein, the author of *Against the Gods: The Remarkable Story of Risk,* was the subject of an interview with Jason Zweig in the November 2004 issue of *Money* magazine. Zweig called him "patience personified," a characterization to which I subscribe. But the best part of this article was Zweig's synopsis of Peter's four "Big Ideas."

1. Anything can happen. We do not and cannot know the future.
2. Whether you should take a risk depends not just on the probability that you are right but also on the consequences if you are wrong.
3. The riskiest moment is when you are right.
4. If you're comfortable with all you own, you're not diversified. Diversification is an explicit recognition of your ignorance.

Marvelous words with which to think about risk management!

Lessons from Denmark and China

What is happening? In the past few months, in both China and Denmark, organizations followed, to a scrupulous degree, the letter of local laws and customs only to find themselves attacked elsewhere in the world. In both cases these attacks were radical and unexpected, well beyond the outer limits of outcomes suggested by conventional econometric and even subjective risk management models.

In the Danish case, a newspaper editor asked artists to draw for publication some deliberately controversial political cartoons, some of which displayed a purported likeness of the Prophet Muhammad. The editor assumed that, living in a country and region in which free speech is recognized as one of its principal liberties, he can be criticized for insensitivity, or even childish behavior, but he won't be hauled into court, nor will property be damaged and lives lost. A few months pass after publication, during which several European papers reprint the cartoons. Then some local Islamic religious leaders travel to the Middle East and deliberately use these drawings to incite the Muslim world into frenzy, leading to riots, the destruction of considerable public and private property, and numerous deaths. Other religious leaders fan the flames. They spread to Iran, Egypt, Libya, Indonesia, Pakistan, Malaysia, Syria, Lebanon and Nigeria, and include marches and riots in Europe. One religious leader suggests that the artists themselves should be murdered and offers cash rewards of up to $11 million! Yet few political leaders in the West had the guts to stand up for free speech, called by *The Economist* "the defining freedom of liberal societies." The result, as succinctly expressed by that newspaper, is "mutual incomprehension, mutual outrage," with continuing violence.

In China, several US corporations, including Microsoft, Yahoo, Cisco and Google, sell hardware, software and services to the Chinese, agreeing to adhere to local Chinese laws in return for the privilege. These laws are at odds with the prevailing North American and European standards of freedom of speech and research, but these companies argue that they are the wedges for more open societies. Almost immediately politicians and rights organizations attacked these corporations, including bringing some of their executives to Washington for an incendiary public hearing. Google's stock price takes a nosedive, losing many billions of dollars in market value, and the reputations of the four companies are tarnished, whether justified or not. The passions of those opposed to the actions of these four companies are only slightly less incensed than those of the religious fanatics on the other side of the world.

The art of risk management is to try and imagine multiple unexpected outcomes, even when they are highly unlikely, preparing our organizations for all contingencies. The lessons of the Danish cartoons and manifestly restrictive and unjust local laws demonstrate that public reactions can easily exceed expectations. Risk officers must prepare their organizations for outliers unimaginable only a few years ago. We live in a day of instant communication and deliberately inflammatory oratory. When passions prevail, logic and rationality are dismissed as irrelevant. David Brooks summarized the problem in *The New York Times* on February 19, 2006: "The fundamental change is that human beings now look less like self-interested individuals and more like socially-embedded products of family and group." We must acknowledge that we may be closer to lemmings than we thought, easily susceptible to waves of herd emotion. Responding with tolerance to others who are manifestly intolerant of almost every aspect of our culture won't work.

In Western culture, women are free and equal to men. In Islam most remain subjugated. We encourage education that presents multiple points-of-view; their madrassahs insist on rote memorization of the Qu'ran and acceptance of shariah law. We celebrate our press, speech and religious freedoms; they mandate but one word, that of Islam. We seek diversity; they seek uniformity. To us, "blasphemy," "a contemptuous or profane act, utterance or writing about God or a sacred entity" doesn't exist anymore; to them it is a call to physical violence!

Yet we must find a way to co-exist without resorting to the steady violence of the past fifteen years. In the United States, we must acknowledge that, in our own history, we are not far removed from similar acts. Picture the Puritans running the Massachusetts Bay Colony in the late 1600s. Women had to cover their heads. They had no vote and were treated as chattels of their husbands and fathers. Their theocratic religious leaders handed out severe penalties for blasphemy. And mass hysteria erupted after accusations against "witches," followed by some being drowned or burned to death. That was only 300 years ago in North America, and after the so-called "Reformation" in Europe! Nor are we immune from lapses today: In the Midwest in 2006, the complaints of religious fundamentalists forced a high school principal to cancel a student performance of Arthur Miller's *The Crucible*, the play based on those same witch hunts. And in Europe, a British historian was sentenced by an Austrian court to three years in jail for alleging in one of his books that the Holocaust never happened. So much for free speech!

I don't see quick and easy solutions to this clash of civilizations and cultures. The conventional remedies (military power, economic growth, education, and tolerance) don't work. David Brooks summed it up neatly: "If the big contest of the 20th century was between planned and free market economies, the big questions of the next century will be understanding how cultures change and can be changed, how social and cultural capital can be nurtured and developed, how destructive cultural conflict can be turned to healthy cultural competition."

In the meantime, while we grapple with these challenges, we must expand our display of the range of unlikely outcomes facing organizations and reinforce our resilience. This means a greater emphasis on humanism, as defined by the late Edward Said, in *Humanism and Democratic Criticism,* as "using one's mind historically and rationally for the purpose of reflective understanding . . . . Humanism is centered upon the agency of human individuality and subjective intuition, rather than on received ideas and approved authority . . . humanism is the only and, I would go so far as saying, the final resistance we have against the inhuman practices and injustices that disfigure human history."

You fundamentalists have turned yourselves into a superpower of dysfunction, demanding our attention week after week. But it is hard to intimidate people forever into silence, to bottle up the conversation, to lock the world into an epic war only you want. While I don't share your rage, I do understand your panic.

David Brooks, "Drafting Hitler," ***The New York Times*****, February 9, 2006**

The Grasshopper versus Chicken Little: Avian Flu

What is your organization doing about the threat of avian flu? Are you a grasshopper, hoping nothing will happen or that medical science and the pharmaceutical industry will develop new vaccines in sufficient quantity to reduce the effects to minor proportions? Or are you a Chicken Little, constantly warning everyone who will listen that the "end is near?" What is it, constant summer or catastrophe?

There is a third way for responsible risk analysts.

New information in November 2006 indicates that the virus A(H5N1) has mutated to become somewhat more infectious based on a limited number of samples taken in Azerbaijan and Iraq. As *The Economist* reported, this discovery is a "cause for concern but not for panic."

Every organization, large and small, governmental, profit-making and nonprofit alike, should have a continuing working committee composed of medical counsel, technology specialists, human resource staff, and senior management tracking the news and modifying planning based on new information. Above all, this group should relay its fresh conclusions not only to the governing board but also to key "investor" groups, including employees and their families. This is the most difficult part as it requires care to present the latest facts in a way that induces confidence in the organization without creating unnecessary fear.

Within the past year many sound articles on the subject have helped risk managers take effective action. *The New York Times* published "Avian Flu: The Uncertain Threat" on March 28, 2006, a fact-filled and sober assessment of the situation as it then existed. It remains both succinct and useful. *Harvard Business Review,* in its Forethought section for May 2006, published a 22 page Special Report, "Preparing for a Pandemic." One conclusion it reached was that "little stands between the best- and worst-case scenarios," and that "should a pandemic emerge, it would become the single greatest threat to business continuity and could remain so for up to 18 months." The ability to adapt will be the key to the survival of an organization's employees, suppliers and customers and ultimately to the organization itself. *HBR* included a two-page Pandemic Planning Checklist for Businesses, brief and most practical (pages 25-26). Then, in November 2006, the *Natural Hazards Observer* published "Preparing for a Flu Epidemic: A Northwest Perspective," written by two officials of Seattle and King County, Washington. It includes the valuable websites of the U. S. Government (*www.pandemicflu.gov/*) and the World Health Organization (*www.who.int/csr/disease/influenza/en/*).

My summary: organizations require multidisciplinary teams, continuing evaluation as new information develops (on both the spread of the disease and breakthroughs in vaccine science), constant reports to governing boards, information to "investor" groups, plus some innovative thinking about how best to continue operations facing potential severe reductions among customers, suppliers and employees. Here again is a chance for risk management to create opportunity where nothing but threat is in sight. Inventing new and innovative means of maintaining both communications and a modest supply of goods or services to these groups may spell the difference between severe retrenchment or bankruptcy and rapid post-pandemic recovery.

Think about it.

On Transparency

In this age of constant and immediate news of political, business and even personal events, what should be the limits of confidentiality and transparency? Late in June I listened to a television debate on the *New York Times* article disclosing that the US government since 2001 has used information from SWIFT on international financial transfers as a method of finding terrorists. The reporter for the *Times* defended his article, arguing it is the natural responsibility of the press to report on governmental actions, especially those appearing to break the law. A Congressman responded that this article hampered the right and responsibility of the government "to protect us." He labeled the article "despicable," and even possibly "treasonous." Similar voices suggest those in power in government "know more" about the world situation than we ordinary citizens and we should always "trust" government to protect us. Emperors, kings, popes, ayatollahs, mullahs, family dons, some presidents and life's self-appointed aristocrats and tyrants use this argument.

Despite being savaged repeatedly by such as Thomas Paine, Fyodor Dostoevsky and George Orwell, this fallacy reappears, especially in times of alleged stress. "We know more than you, so trust us." "All animals are equal, but some are more equal than others." This argument always begins the end of liberty, of freedom, and independent thought. Robert Oppenheimer summarized this essential idea in an article in 1950 (quoted by Kai Bird and Martin Sherwin in their *American Prometheus)* "The relevant facts could be of little help to an enemy; yet they are indispensable for an understanding of questions of policy."

Transparency of information is the essential cornerstone of that liberty, never to be sacrificed under any circumstances, even if it seems to some that our "security" may be compromised. Does the same precept apply to the private sector? I think it does. As in the public sector, trust is the goal, an equal cornerstone of economic freedom. I've argued for some time that complete and full disclosure of information on the major risks faced by organizations to a broad constituency, other than just internal management and the governing board, is an essential prerequisite for good stakeholder risk management. Using the arguments "they won't and can't understand," "the information will be misused," and "they should trust us" is as improper as asking voters to accept blindly the decisions of their leaders. It is too easy to (using the words of another *Times* article) "substitute easily grasped absolutes for messy and ambiguous realities." We must work harder to be understood. The challenge is to deliver more and better information, in an intelligible form, to stakeholders.

It is all about trust, a critical and elusive relationship.

And how should we treat the information we are given? The words attributed to Ronald Reagan are the best: "Trust but verify!"

> The prospect of acquired perfection lies behind many big ideas and most bad ones. If you do the right thing, believe the right thing, suffer enough, kill enough of the wrong people or breed enough of the right ones—then you will end up in paradise. That is a great motivator, often with awful results . . . . Trying to transcend our own imperfections, rather than eradicating those of others, is the best bet . . . .
>
> **From "Positing Paradise," *The Economist,* July 1, 2006**

CHAPTER 11

Executive Compensation and Apologies

For some years I've commented on the rapacious greed and arrogance shown by some executive officers and their compliant directors, and the abject failure of most risk officers to do anything to try and correct the situation. Add to that the inability of almost anyone to offer a proper apology when responsible for a foul-up. Here are three connected essays.

> (Bosses) are a bit like medieval knights granted great tracts of land by grateful monarchs. It was always too much to expect them to say, "Thank you, milud, but the little cottage by the main gate will do me nicely." Or, indeed, at some later date to suggest: "Since I just lost that battle, here's half my land back."
>
> **"Fat Cats Feeding," *The Economist,* October 11, 2003**

Excessive Executive Compensation

I've thumped my drum too often over the failure of most American organizations to do anything of substance to restrain executive compensation, something that reaches lemming-like insanity. It is creeping into Canada, Australia and Europe and may well become as virulent a disease as consumer litigation. I first harangued readers on this problem in mid-2001, then in January 2002 and again, in greater detail, in August 2002. My point then, as now, is that trust in an organization is the keystone on which its future is built. It is more critical to corporate survival than any form of assets or earnings. It is an edifice of perception, painstakingly built and easily destroyed, when a tide of fresh public opinion washes away its underpinnings. Trust and reputation are one and the same and, as I've argued since the mid-1990s, building and maintaining this trust is the single-most important goal for risk management.

The biggest question is how and what a risk officer can or should do to convince a governing board of the long-term downside effects of excessive executive pay? In 2002, one manager wrote me: "To think that the risk management community can/should influence corporate governance, especially executive compensation, is . . . well, just naïve." He was right: he was an insurance manager, with "risk management" in his title, positioned below middle management. To raise this question in his corporation would have meant immediate walking papers. Yet the failure of anyone inside to address a situation that threatens an entire organization is why so many larger companies have come to grief recently. The "risk management community" has grown in the past four years. Chief Risk Officers are common, and many have direct reporting relationships to their boards. To deny responsibility is a craven form of avoiding accountability.

It should be a bit easier in 2006. The U.S. Securities & Exchange Commission has enacted new and tighter requirements for reporting the amounts of executive pay (at least for publicly-traded operations), from "golden hellos" (signing bonuses) and "golden parachutes," to salaries, annual bonuses, stock options, and the other, often hidden, perks (club dues, limos and drivers, tax payments, etc.) showered on our executives. Disclosure, however, is only a first. We have research analyses showing how far off kilter we are. *The Economist* (October 11, 2003) reported "in 1980, the average pay for the CEOs of America's biggest companies was about 40 times that of the average production worker. In 1990, it was about 85 times. Now (2003) this ratio is thought to be about 400." On January 18, 2006, *The New York Times* cited two sources showing that the ratio of average chief executive compensation to average worker pay had risen from 100 in 1990 to a peak of over 500 in 2000, slipping back to 300 in 2002 and increasing again in 2004 to over 400. Are our CEOs of 2006 any wiser or more capable than those of 1990? I doubt it. The press reels with new adjectives describing this greed: "outsized," "obscene," "bloated," "absurd," and "outrageous." These payments are also cheating shareholders, according to a new study by Lucien Bebchuk, at Harvard. He reports that, from 2000 to 2003, "the total compensation of the five best-paid officers of all publicly held companies amounted to ten percent of corporate earnings." Joseph Nocera, in *The New York Times,* wrote "We know that it (executive compensation) is out of control, socially corrosive and divorced from any real rationale."

Yet will these new disclosure rules have any real effect? Some cynics say no. They argue that all this new information will simply raise the bar once again as compensation committees, executives and their consultants point to the new information to push for yet higher levels, so that no one is being paid "less than average!" Right after the announcement of the new SEC regulations, UAL Corporation (United Airlines), seeking to emerge from bankruptcy, baldly approved a pay package for its executives that combined higher salaries with stock incentives of more than $115 million! How do they think the UAL employees, suppliers, customers, and creditors are likely to respond?

Fortunately there are a few signs of moderation and reason. Morningstar Inc. named Rich Kinder, the CEO of Kinder Morgan Inc. as its "chief executive of the year." Why? He accepts a salary of US$1 a year and takes as his reward only the dividends payable on his stock from the company's earnings (that his dividends were about $18 million in the third quarter of 2005 may be immaterial!). His company's dividends are concrete results of performance, going to *all* shareholders. Not all CEOs can or do hold that much stock in their organizations but the publicity attached to this announcement may cause some reflection by compensation committees.

One of my readers complained that many of the strident complaints of over-paid executives come from a narrow coterie of misanthropic journalists, academics and NGOs congenitally opposed to "corporations" *per se*. Perhaps. He also acknowledged a "strong personal bias" as he too would love to be so munificently overpaid. That's his personal challenge to keep working. Here's my answer.

First, we must deal with perceptions, as distorted and irrational as we believe them to be. The world of perception is the world of reality. The CEO is the leader of any organization, and, as such, any publicity about the leader reflects on the organization (rightly or wrongly) and affects the confidence of stakeholders. Logically, CEO compensation matters, especially when its ratio to that of the average worker is so out of whack.

Second, the reputation of shareholder-owned corporations varies from one period and one country to another. In the developed world, corporations in general do not now hold a high degree of public support. Some do (Apple, for example) but most don't. It's not rational, and certainly unfair, but that's the current perception. It's the environment in which a risk officer must operate and it affects both strategic and tactical decisions. Perhaps it's unfair that some NGOs, media, and activists paint corporations as greedy, environmentally unresponsive monsters, but it is an uncomfortable fact.

Third, most humans are economic animals, and monetary incentives move us to action. We relish large financial rewards, but when do rewards exceed rationality? And, given the behavior of many executives after receiving larger than life rewards (like winning the lottery), I argue that excessive rewards often lead to misfortune and sorrow! Instead of annual bonuses, why not relate them to a running five-year performance average? Why not require executives to hold their stock and options until resignation or retirement, including a mandatory divestiture of a major portion if they are sacked for cause?

Fourth, I do not propose setting an absolute limit on executive compensation nor support laws that do this. That makes no sense. What I do propose is that rational risk analysis suggests that some degree of proportionality of executive pay to average worker wages makes sense for both the organization internally and its public stakeholders, particularly at this moment. If 40 times average worker pay gave us good management in the early 1990s, why did we allow it to explode to over 400 in the early 2000s? Excessive executive compensation may lead to a reduction in stakeholder confidence as well as inappropriate executive behavior. What should guide a Board and its compensation committee? The guide must be a *balance* between an enterprise's stimulation created by generous rewards and a reduction in its reputation connected to excessive rewards. Too little reward and you lose effective leaders and managers; too much and you lose your reputation. As times and general perceptions change, so should the responses of governing boards change.

Creativity and innovation are not always the result of higher financial rewards: some of us are moved by intellectual challenge, or altruism, or simple curiosity, or money. We should take into account all these stimuli, plus the view of the stake holding public.

As I wrote in both 2002 and 2006, re-establishing trust for an organization among critical stakeholders and the public continues as the single-most important risk management goal. As a risk officer you *must* raise the issue of executive compensation, no matter how sweaty your palms!

When little or nothing is done, I'm forced to return to this topic.

More on Reputation and Executive Compensation

Why are organizations so willing to trash their reputations and so reluctant to permit any volatility in published earnings? This is a risk management conundrum. Of course, reputation is difficult to measure while earnings are guided by numerous accounting rules and regulations. In this era of the ascendancy of bean counters, perhaps I should not be surprised.

Take the situation of excessive executive compensation, one fouling the reputation of numerous corporations, not only in North America but also now in Europe. I wrote about this problem in January 2006 and it deteriorates every day. The word "obscene" is an understatement! Consider this litany of greed reported in the press:

- UnitedHealth grants its CEO a windfall in stock options of $1.6 *billion;*
- Pfizer, with a falling stock price, pays its CEO $65 million from 2001 to 2005 and adds an $83 million pension;
- Exxon-Mobil gives its exiting CEO almost $400 million;
- Verizon in 2005, in the face of a 5% drop in its stock price and a 25% reduction in earnings still paid its CEO $48 million;
- Home Depot, its stock down 12%, managed to award its CEO $245 million, and now faces allegations of backdating; and
- Fannie Mae may undergo a criminal investigation for fiddling its accounting so that its executives drew substantially more in compensation than they were due.

European executives, watching this flood of excess across the Pond, are following suit. A recent study of compensation shows that the median CEO pay is $6.8 million in the United States and $4.3 million in Europe. Only eight years ago it was $1.1 million in Europe. Are European CEOs four times more valuable in eight years? The ratio of average CEO pay to the average pay of ordinary workers was around 200 to 250 up to

1997, but leapt beyond 400 in the past few years, topping 525 in 2000 and only receding to 431 in 2004 (Source: Institute for Policy Studies/United for a Fair Economy). A study from *CFO* magazine (May 2006) reports that 34% of CFOs believe *their own* CEOs are "very to somewhat overpaid!"

Executive perks are also out of control and attracting attention. The backdating of options is a mounting disgrace, with more than 100 companies under investigation. Corporate jets ferry executives not only to business appointments but also to posh resorts and golfing sites, often with friends, families and compliant politicians. Corporations pay extravagant dues of clubs around the world. They even pay the taxes that their execs must cough up for their excessive compensation!

Is anyone in control? Many CEOs surround themselves on their boards with compliant peers, willing to scratch backs for higher income. Compensation committees hire consulting firms to study and benchmark prevailing pay levels. They then suggest that all of their clients are indeed "above average," (the Lake Wobegon Syndrome) and recommend "above average" pay. Meanwhile corporate reputations sink even lower as stakeholders react with cynicism and lack of confidence. Where are our Chief Risk Officers in this mess? Many are so enmeshed with their econometric models that they neglect the downside risks of excessive compensation. Others quake at challenging either an exec or the board, fearing immediate redundancy. It is the "silence of the lambs."

This practice of excessive executive compensation, far beyond the limits considered rational, erodes that trust and confidence so essential to an effective and efficient market economy. It creates a public perception of unbridled greed. A June 2006 Watson Wyatt study showed that both corporate directors and institutional investors agreed (79% and 85%) that the current pay model "has hurt corporate America's image" and that companies "have dramatically overpaid executives" (61% and 90%). Some argue that this inequality is an essential part of a market economy, to create challenge for other, "underpaid" mortals. They say they need a carrot to stimulate productivity and innovation. Perhaps, but have our innovative abilities and productivity increased at the same pace as recent compensation inflation?

What are some of the possible solutions?

First, generally accepted by most observers, is the creation of a truly independent compensation board committee. No "pals" of the CEO. No directors who serve on more than three other boards. Directors who reflect the interests of both shareholders *and* other stakeholders are critical to the long-term success of every organization.

Second, corporations must disclose more about all forms of executive compensation. The Securities & Exchange Commission in the United States mandated such disclosure in its January 2006 statement. Some skeptics, however, suggest this will merely result in higher compensation as boards apply their own regression to the mean! Greater transparency will at least allow the press and shareholder groups to champion change.

Third, most experts agree that pay for performance must be the mantra, but the key is *how* we *measure* "performance." Warren Buffett, a director at Coca Cola, encourages the use of a three to five year running average of earnings (not stock prices subject to external variables, plus and minus). Measuring performance over a longer time period is essential.

Fourth, a compensation committee should select some measure on internal pay equity in relation to other employees. A ratio of average executive compensation to average production worker compensation would establish a guide. I'd like to see a return to a ratio not in excess of 200 but it may take some time to return to that level of rationality. J. Pierpont Morgan was alleged to have said he would not lend to a company whose CEO was paid more than 40 times the average of the lowest staff. This should be a *guide* only, one that can and should be exceeded under unusual circumstances. It never should be the subject of law or regulation. If we fail to correct the situation ourselves, we may have the politicians on our backs.

Fifth, and finally, an organization needs a strong ERM program and an equally strong and *independent* Chief Risk Officer, one who reports directly to the Board, willing to report the emperor has no clothes when he is indeed naked! Risk Officers must take responsibility for this problem.

The reputation of an organization is difficult to measure, yet it remains the cornerstone of its resilience when facing adverse situations. More than any other single individual, a CEO's personal habits, attitudes, and communication skills affect this reputation. When a CEO steps over the line, as many have done with their compensation, someone must be there to ask, as Joseph Welch did of Senator McCarthy in the 1954 Army-McCarthy hearings, "Have you no decency, sir? At long last, have you no sense of decency?" Ben Stein reminded me of this quote in his column in *The New York Times* on December 8, 2005, and it is a fitting conclusion to this discussion.

> Obfuscation is rife in three areas in particular—pensions, perks and deferred pay.
>
> ***The Economist,* January 21, 2006**

If, finally, someone will acknowledge that compensation is out of control, perhaps we will hear an apology. Unfortunately, the art of apology seems to be non-existent today.

Update on Apologies

Over the years I've considered the nature and importance of the apology not only as a condition precedent for a civil society but also as a means of undercutting the rampant run of unnecessary litigation that epitomizes the United States of late. In 1988 I read an article by two Boston doctors on "Apologizing to Patients" that emphasized the significance of acknowledging human relationships. They pointed out that "the illusion of certainty is one that is cherished by both physician and patient because it tends to diminish anxiety and support the feeling of control." Of course, "certainty" is seldom the outcome, and they went on: "Apology, as we are suggesting, is a respectful invitation to shared mourning over a loss of certainty, perfection, and one's high hopes . . . . (It) is an acknowledgement of the reality of regret and tragedy." I concluded that quote with my own comment: "Prompt and understanding acknowledgment of fault, including an offer to provide immediate help in attempting to rectify the situation to the extent possible, will reduce the hurt and the normal feelings of vindictiveness toward the person or organization possibly responsible for the injury."

Thirteen years later, in 2001, I continued these thoughts after the captain of a US Navy submarine profusely apologized to the families of Japanese fishermen killed and injured when his boat surfaced and inadvertently destroyed their fishing vessel. That expression of contrition jarred many Americans, used to the admonitions of lawyers and insurers to say nothing and admit nothing, in order to avoid plaintiffs' counsel using such statements as admissions of guilt. I pointed out at that time that accepting responsibility did not necessarily amount to an admission of guilt.

It's sad that we appear to have lost our ability to express contrition, commiseration, and responsibility in many walks of life. The now-standard evasion of politicians—"mistakes were made," that shocking passive attempt to sidestep the buck—can be heard almost weekly, and it has crept into the vernacular of corporate leaders. A recent notable exception was the blunt personal acceptance of responsibility by Warren Buffett a few years ago when he took the personal blame for that year's disappointing results of Berkshire Hathaway.

I was reminded of this while re-reading (the third time) Patrick O'Brian's *Post Captain,* in which early 19th century apologies are effusively offered and generously accepted. The ship's surgeon, Stephen Maturin, says to the ship's lieutenant: "I regret that there has been this misunderstanding. I regret the remarks that passed between us; and if you wish I will repeat my apology on the quarterdeck, before those who heard them." Two hundred years ago apologies were lucid and complete. Of course, to do otherwise might mean facing your opponent early one morning on the Field of Honor, with sword or pistol.

Contrast that with the vernacular today, as illustrated in Robert MacNeil's latest Public Television dissertation on American slang. An apology today is simply, "My bad!" Doesn't this contraction miss much of the importance of reaching out to an injured party? Where is the commiseration? Yes, "my bad" may express responsibility but it hardly redresses the situation. It's almost an invitation to a plaintiff's lawyer!

So today, when we need expressions of apology, humility, and responsibility to begin to defuse the latent animosity in our political and corporate lives, all we get are those passive monstrosities "mistakes were made" and the sports abbreviation "my bad." Perhaps we should all start re-reading those who wrote in and about the 18th and early 19th century.

CHAPTER 12

The Fox and the Hedgehog

I devoted each January issue of Risk Management Reports *to a discussion of the major issues facing the discipline. This chapter is from January 2006.*

> Nothing is really *balanced.* Try to think of it as an ongoing poker game, say five-card draw, but everything constantly changes—the money, the card suits, the players, even the table, and every ante is affected by the weather, and you're playing in a room where the house around you is being demolished.
>
> **Annie Proulx, *Bad Dirt,* Scribner, New York 2004**

Some years ago I read Michael Ignatieff's probing biography of Isaiah Berlin, which, in turn, led me to Berlin's famous essay on the hedgehog and the fox. As I look forward to the twelve months of 2006, I find one big issue and many smaller ones, describing the problem first posed by the Greek poet Archilochus: "the fox knows many things, but the hedgehog knows one big thing." Which course should we take: like the hedgehog, focus with determination on a single "big issue," or like the fox, use flexibility and cunning to respond to the multiple less important issues in the belief that solving these problems will, in itself, solve the big issue?

The hedgehog's issue for 2006 is the same one I described in January 2005. We haven't made much progress. It is *re-establishing the trust and confidence of organizational stakeholders*. The erosion of trust continued in 2005. First, three major disasters hit this earth: the Indonesian tsunami, the rash of hurricanes in the Caribbean and southern United States, and the South Asia earthquakes. The global and national responses were both unprecedented and inadequate, revealing unanticipated weaknesses. Are we capable of mounting an effective relief effort? Second, governments around the world are less trusted than ever before, in light of outright mendacity, corruption and duplicitous conduct. Throwing "the rascals" out is a common reaction, especially in South America. Is there any politician whose words you can trust? Given the disclosures in 2005 about the underhanded payments to supposedly objective writers to support particular viewpoints, generally those of parties in power, all we can do is become more cynical about political institutions. Third, nonprofits and NGOs demonstrate their own signs of fallibility. The failure of the American Red Cross, among others, to govern itself responsibly creates doubt among its donors as to its ability to serve the public. The efforts of religious ideologues to force non-scientific ideas into the science curricula in states such as Kansas and Pennsylvania erode trust in our educational system. And fourth, profit-making institutions continue to undermine their public support with unwarranted practices. Excessive executive pay, especially in the United States, defies belief! In this country, in 2004, the ratio of average executive pay to that of the average production worker *increased* from just less than 300 to over 400, striving to return to the absurd 500+ ratio reached in 1999 and 2000 and in blatant contrast to the 100 ratio in 1990. As Ben Stein noted in *The New York Times* on December 18, 2005, "executives gone wild: it's not a pretty sight . . . . I'm a devout capitalist, but this is just plain ugly." No wonder corporations have public relations problems, when their executives show outright greed every day. It is the responsibility of boards to rein in these excesses, but so far they have failed to act. Each board wants to pay its senior executive something more than "the average," leading to the Lake Wobegone syndrome described by Garrison Keillor where "all the children are above average." This compensation problem is terrible publicity. It destroys employee morale and it cheats shareholders. Some years ago I suggested that so-called "risk managers" should make this their most important target, only to have numerous readers tell me that to do so would be tantamount to job suicide. They may be right, but who is going to stop this rush to corporate self-destruction? This is another reason to support the job of CRO, someone who reports not only to the CEO but also to the Board. We need a manager with a degree of independence. With unrestrained executive compensation undermining public trust, how can this not be a paramount risk management issue? And then we have the continuing walk of the executive perpetrators to court and jail. I've written at length about the blatant conflicts of interest that riddle the financial services arena, including stock analysts fiddling their reviews to favor well-heeled corporate clients, mutual funds permitting late trading to special clients (Bear Stearns paid a $250 million settlement in December 2005), and insurance brokers taking egregious payments from their vendors. This "what's in it for me" disease has now crept into medical services, with the disclosure that behind-the scenes payments are corrupting both medical research and healthcare. Paul Krugman, writing in *The New York Times* on December 16, 2005, concludes "The essence is simple: crucial scientific research and crucial medical decisions have to be considered suspect because of financial ties among medical companies, medical researchers and health care providers." He went on: "The point is that the whiff of corruption in our medical system isn't emanating from a few bad apples. The whole system of incentives encourages doctors and researchers to serve the interests of the medical industry."

He's right in focusing on incentives: from stockbrokers, pension advisors, and mutual funds to insurance brokers and medical professionals, skewed incentives inevitably create opportunities for self-dealing that, when they are inevitably disclosed, undermine public confidence.

So restoring public confidence, the support of an entire stakeholder group, is and must be the primary goal of risk management in 2006 (and beyond). Reviewing executive compensation and skewed incentives are only two of the steps responsible risk managers must take. A good hedgehog will focus steadfastly on this issue, almost to the exclusion of all others.

So what of the fox, who sees a multitude of connected issues, "often unrelated and contradictory" as Isaiah Berlin called them? We must address them, mustn't we? On the pessimistic side, we have the threat of avian flu that could be the long-forecast global pandemic. The World Health Organization suggests that, at its worst, it could debilitate up to 25% of a region's total workforce at one time, bringing economic chaos. The medics already acknowledge that we are far short of any vaccine that could help reduce the contagion and, as well, the medicines that could be used to treat patients. Given that the world experiences a pandemic two or three times a century, we must be prepared in some way. It is called "risk management for the highest stakes" (*The New York Times,* November 25, 2005). One company, Lehman Brothers, the New York financial firm in that already experienced a facility shutdown following 9/11, has responded to the avian flu threat with a study of health, technology and industry implications, using a team of technology executives, doctors and managers. Could many of its employees work from home? Could competitors link themselves together to avert financial panic? Sound risk management requires an assessment of the potential consequences and ripple effects of an event, followed by possible actions to reduce adverse effects and even enhance a competitive position. Above all, continued consultation with key stakeholder groups can create that re-assurance essential to continuity.

The fox must consider other issues. Growing confirmation that human activities accelerate global warming means increasing pressure to act, not only at the national but also at the corporate level. Scientists now believe in a causal connection between warming and the increased frequency and severity of windstorms. Population growth is still out of control is many developing areas. The increased demand for potable water threatens political upheavals. And in both the United States and the Middle East we watch the last gasp (I hope) of reactionary religious advocates who try to stifle the scientific process. Tenzin Gyatso, the current and 14th Dalai Lama, made a remarkable observation on the relationship between science and religion: "If science proves some belief in Buddhism wrong, then Buddhism will have to change. In my view, science and Buddhism share a search for the truth and for understanding reality. By learning from science about aspects of reality where its understanding may be more advanced, I believe that Buddhism enriches its own worldview." Can we possibly convince other religious leaders, from imams, ayatollahs and Popes, to priests, pastors, rabbis, and comrades, to come to such an enlightened view?

Of course, the fox must also contend with a host of conventional risk issues, ranging from foreign exchange fluctuation, market volatility and creditworthiness to myriad questions in the operational sector. For many risk managers these are so all-encompassing that they have no time to consider these larger issues, much less the focus of the hedgehog.

Above all, don't disregard the more optimistic developments, unexpected events with a more favorable outcome than anticipated. The December vote in Iraq may be the beginning of progress in the Middle East, just as we've seen a remarkable change in the Balkans ten years after initial intervention. The economic progress of both India and China could infect the rest of Asia and the Middle East. The current high prices of energy might stimulate more study and investment in alternative sources. Unintended and unexpected consequences rattle our complacencies for both good and ill.

I note with some amusement the saber rattling of Hugo Chavez in Venezuela. He has threatened to interrupt shipments of oil to the United States, because, as he says, he thinks President Bush intends to invade his country. Here's an example of a self-fulfilling prophecy!

What is your choice for 2006? Adopt the single-minded emphasis on restoring stakeholder confidence in your organization, like the hedgehog, or take arms against the multiplicity of risks, from the global to the mundane, in the hope that being fleet of foot and flexible will enable your organization to stay ahead of the pack. Can we be both fox and hedgehog?

I have more good news for 2006: the ideas of sound risk management are beginning to infiltrate all levels of management and the economy. The Royal Society of Arts in London is conducting a three-year study of risk and risk management. New York University (among other educational institutions around the world) offers a course in integrated risk management. A new Geneva think tank called the International Risk Governance Council (IRGC) just published a reflective analysis of an integrative approach to "risk governance." An Economist Intelligence Unit survey of global practices in risk management reveals that our discipline's ideas are being adopted within many organizations. And the International Standards Organization has initiated a study leading to a new international "standard" on risk management, to be published in 2008.

Consider some other indications that intelligent risk design is taken seriously.

1. *On Uncertainty* Two recent articles warrant comment. The first, "In Praise of Uncertainty," by Jonathan Zittrain, in the May 2005 issue of *Harvard Business Review,* suggests that the explosion of information technology was fuelled by the lack of knowledge of which products and services would succeed. The author sees *uncertainty* as a positive and dynamic incentive rather than a deterrent to innovation. It's another argument why I think we should relish this idea. The second is "Living with Uncertainty," by James Davison Hunter, in *INSight,* Fall 2005, from the Institute for Advance Studies in Culture (University of Virginia). "Uncertainty is an issue for the entire culture (with) enormous consequences (and) difficult challenges," he argues, going on that "the great promise of the Enlightenment of the 17th and 18th centuries was that by reason alone we could attain truth—a truth beyond the reach of doubt, free from the prejudices of subjectivity and essential to a life worth living." When we didn't achieve "certainty," some began to doubt everything and others resorted to

religious and secular "fundamentalisms," ideas that profess a new certainty. Too many of us cannot yet accept that uncertainty is a human stimulant. We want to resolve it by translating a portion of it into "risk," using bases of collected information and econometric models that give semblances of certitude, or by accepting the dogma of some external guru. Both these options are illusions. The first can help us decide more intelligently while the second absolves us of any personal decision-making at all. Only be accepting uncertainty as a stimulant and aggressively accepting it we can make any progress.

2. *Information Brief on International Risk Management Standards* This is a well-researched and challenging paper on risk management by Marc Saner, published by the Institute on Governance, in Ottawa, Canada (www.iog.ca). Saner reviews current national standards in Australia, New Zealand, the United States, and UK, plus the recent work of the IOS and the IRGC. His appendices are especially valuable resources. He confirms that our discipline "is still in rapid development" and that, although "at a basic level it is very simple and intuitive," it invites organizations to try and "reinvent" it. The recent efforts of COSO and ISO illustrate this. Too many "reinventions" lead to confusion rather than clarification. He also warns that some segments of risk management are constrained by existing domestic and international legislation, practices, and trade agreements where definitions appear to be cast in concrete, thus restricting the evolution of our discipline.
3. *Risk Governance: Towards an Integrative Approach* This white paper, from the IRGC (see note above) in Geneva (*www.irgc.org*) is clearly a "public policy sector" analysis of our discipline, one crafted primarily by adherents of the Society for Risk Analysis. Written by Dr. Ortwin Renn, with annexes by Peter Graham, it has only minor input from the financial risk management sectors represented by GARP, PRMIA and the SOA. It recommends adding the "societal context" in risk management decisions, something I've supported for many years, and suggests a new "categorization of risk-related knowledge." In the first area it encourages an understanding of "the structure and interplay of the different actors dealing with risks, how these actors may differently perceive the risks and what concerns they have regarding their likely consequences." Its 66 pages are dense in some areas but worth study. I won't try to condense its ideas: instead, order a copy and read it. The annexes in this paper are valuable for comparative analyses of existing guidelines, regulations, definitions, and standards.

I have, at the start of this year, first a hedgehog's conviction that one overweening issue, trust, is the critical challenge. It is conflicted with a fox's view of multiple risk issues, each of which commands attention. In a sense this is absurd but perhaps we all need a sense of the ridiculous to save us from self-importance. Isaiah Berlin once again: "What presumptuous nonsense it is to claim to perceive an order merely on the strength of believing desperately that an order must exist, when all one actually perceives is meaningless chaos—a chaos of which the heightened form, the microcosm in which the disorder of human life is reflected, is war." Is this too cynical? Can we actually tame uncertainty? No, but risk management can give us a better sense of possible outcomes. When and if a cataclysmic event occurs, will we be prepared? Preparation is less a matter of spending enormous sums for levees, early-warning systems, intrusive intelligence, or insurance, and more of psychological awareness and resilience. This leads directly to the confidence of organizational stakeholders that we can survive and even prosper after any event. Berlin writes, "tragedy is intrinsic to choice and we are doomed to choose, and every choice may entail an irreparable loss," (I'd add the possibility of benefit and victory!). Accept this uncertainty with profound good humor. A famous Zen koan demonstrates that the apparently ridiculous is profound: "what is the sound of one hand clapping?"

Humor and a sense of the ridiculous should also skewer self-importance! Too much of what I read in risk management is a waste of time and words, and perhaps my own musings fall in the same category. I continue to relish, however, the critiques with which I agree. Gardiner Morse (*Harvard Business Review,* November 2005) uses the word "crap" when he critiques those ubiquitous "circles" so often seen in Power Point presentations: step one leads to further steps that complete the circle with step one again. Morse calls these "crap" circles that bear no relation to reality. What really happens is a spin into a new circle. John Adams, the author of *Risk,* uses an identical acronym for "Compulsive Risk Assessment Psychosis" (CRAP) to describe much of the pseudo-science that tries to attach horrendous results to shallow risk assessments (such as "electromagnetic hypersensitivity" for alleged symptoms of people living near high-transmission electric lines). The symptoms may be real but there is as yet no scientific evidence for causal relativity.

My coda to "crap" ends with the superb analysis by Harry Frankfurt, professor at Princeton, entitled *On Bullshit* (Princeton University Press, Princeton 2005). "The essence of bullshit is not that it is false but that it is phony . . . . But the mode of creativity upon which it relies is less analytical and less deliberative than that which is mobilized in lying. It is more expansive and independent, with more spacious opportunities for improvisation, color, and imaginative play. This is less a matter of craft than of art." So Professor Frankfurt concludes: "sincerity itself is bullshit."

I end this dissertation on issues for 2006 on this excremental note, much the same as I did in 2005.

> People are sick of bullshit; they're starved for truth, they're starved for straight talk, for somebody who will come in and tell things the way they are."
>
> **Harry G. Frankfurt, *On Bullshit,***
> **Princeton University Press, Princeton 2005**

CHAPTER 13

Some Musings on Risk Management

> Here's my final puzzle: in a world that is clearly going down the tubes, where the forces of barbarism are on the march and the forces of civilization cannot stop them, why don't we all spend a large part of every day being grateful for where we are?
>
> **Ben Stein, "My Country, Right and Wrong (but Why So Wrong?),** ***The New York Times,*** **August 6, 2006**

Each day managers make decisions for their organizations based on past experience, limited information about the future and their hoped-for results. Despite the most sophisticated analyses, the future always surprises us. Good news: Joan Kroc leaves \$1.5 *billion* to The Salvation Army in the US, a bequest surpassing the \$1 billion that Ted Turner donated to the United Nations. Bad news: the Roman Catholic Church in both Europe and North America is submerged in a tidal wave of allegations of sexual abuse. Both situations are deviations from what we, internal managers and external stakeholders, have been led to expect. One is remarkably favorable, the other terribly destructive. Both are examples of risk, a measure of the possibility of an unexpected result. When we depart on our courses after making fresh decisions, we must recognize the broad range of possible alternative outcomes and consequences, well beyond those that we hope and expect to materialize. Constructing those alternative outcomes and being prepared for them is the art of risk management.

The discipline of risk management is an evolution of common sense. Human beings have always taken their experiences and constructed potential futures based on what they knew or thought they knew. In the absence of concrete examples, they often resorted to the forecasts of oracles, and when, that wasn't enough, they made prayers, sacrifices and donations to their gods of choice. Uncertainty was the major ingredient in decision-making and faith in some superior being was often the only recourse. Over the centuries, however, the search for new knowledge combined with the ability to record what went before led to enlightened individuals who began to construct quantitative probabilities for possible consequences. The story of our ability to construct a measure of the possibility of various outcomes—what we now call risk—can be found in Peter Bernstein's classic *Against the Gods: The Remarkable Story of Risk.*

It is the chronicle of our centuries-old progress from reliance on guesswork and the gods to transforming at least some uncertainty into something more concrete through the application of experience, numbers and probability.

Bernstein writes: "The revolutionary idea that defines the boundary between modern times and the past is the mastery of risk: the notion that the future is more than a whim of the gods and that men and women are not passive before nature. Until human beings discovered a way across that boundary, the future was a mirror of the past or a murky domain of oracles and soothsayers who held a monopoly over knowledge of anticipated events."

His book describes the efforts of well-known trailbreakers such as Pascal, Fermat, Edward Lloyd, Bernoulli, Bayes, and Bentham. He also introduces us to many less—known names such as Pisano (Arabic numerals), Cardano (probabilities of dice), John Graunt (statistical tables), Abraham de Moivre (the "bell" curve and standard deviation), and Francis Galton (regression to the mean).

We've made even more progress in measuring and understanding risk in the past century. Consider such milestones as Frank Knight's *Risk, Uncertainty & Profit* (1921), which celebrated the prevalence of surprise and separated risk from uncertainty, John Maynard Keynes' *Treatise on Probability* (1921), which cited the importance of perception and introduced us to the Law of Great Numbers, Von Neumann and Morgenstern (1926 and 1953), who created the theory of games and strategy and suggested that the goal of not losing is often superior to that of winning, Markowitz (1952), who developed portfolio analysis, including new aspects of returns and variances, and Daniel Kahneman and Amos Tversky, who published their "prospect theory" in 1979, demonstrating that human nature can be perversely irrational, especially in the face of risk, and that the fear of loss often trumps the hope of gain.

We now have a fresh appreciation of risk itself: a measure of the possibility of deviation from the expected. Yet with the cascade of new ideas and mathematical models, too many of today's practitioners of risk management look at it in a limited fashion. Three problems remain unresolved. First, they see risk as a negative result, a loss, a downside outcome, and, in so doing, they unnecessarily limit their responses. Second, as too many tacticians see risk management as a practice restricted to their own limited area of expertise, be it credit management, security, safety, hedging or insurance. And third, the goal of risk management is too restricted.

First, consider 'risk" itself. Any decision, be it personal or organizational, is based on a perception of resulting benefits and negative consequences. When I cross the street against a red light, I consciously and subconsciously weigh my potential benefits (I can save perhaps 45 seconds in reaching my ultimate destination) against possible mishaps (injury or even death from a speeding car I didn't see; a ticket from a passing police officer). My risk analysis says that the probability of the benefit is very high (close to 100%) while the probabilities of the negative results are very low (less than 2%). While my assessments of these probabilities are almost certainly wrong, they are the basis for my decision. Rationally I should reconsider the extremes of the downside results (death?) and the modest benefit, and wait until the light turns green, but human beings do not always act rationally with risk, as Kahneman and Tversky illustrated! Consider another example. When you buy a lottery ticket, the odds of losing your investment are incredibly high and those of winning the grand prize infinitesimally small, yet fools buy these tickets every day. The enormity of the favorable consequence is an irresistible lure that numbs rational thinking. We can apply the same analysis to plunging into stocks at the height of a bull market, rather than cautiously investing for the long haul.

When we make a decision in an organization, the sources and volume of information are far more complex, as are the outcomes that can be modified by both global and local reactions. In addition personal desires and predilections warp our perspectives. We tend to upgrade the probabilities of favorable outcomes and downgrade negative outcomes solely because we've invested time and money in an idea. We thus become "gamblers," not investors. This behavior crops up every day at the gambling casinos, where rationality is submerged beneath the lure of great gains on the next roll of the dice. The reverse also corrupts our decision-making. We can be so afraid of losing even a small portion of what we now have that we become irrationally averse to any downside result, trapping us in inactivity and lethargy.

Thus "risk" itself must always encompass a reasonably rational assessment of all potential outcomes, both favorable and unfavorable. Risk analysis must always look intelligently on the magnitude of various consequences relative to our current position.

So while elements of the art of risk management are bandied about almost daily in our organizations today, we still have difficulty in understanding the nature of risk. Too often we fail to recognize the potential benefits that accrue from taking risk.

Second, we define "risk management" too narrowly. It is a discipline for dealing with uncertainty, a more rigorous and intelligent application of knowledge and experience to pulling aside some of the curtains of the unknown future. Yet, in a sense, "risk management" is a misnomer. We never "manage" risk. We can only measure the possibility of alternative outcomes and, using that information, manage our organizations with this new knowledge. Risk exists in the nature of things, only a portion of which we can ever understand. Within organizations, too many tacticians try to capture the idea of risk management for their chosen practice, refusing to admit that others use the same general practice and that cooperation and collaboration rather than competition, will improve strategic results. On the broad organizational level, the discipline should be part of the daily thought processes of every stakeholder, from employees and managers to investors, suppliers and customers. It is not the private preserve of a credit risk analyst, or a derivatives trader, or a safety director, or an insurance buyer. All have something to contribute to the sum total of risk information but no one is the "risk manager."

Third, the goal of risk management is corrupted. Too much of the writings of advisors, commentators and consultants in the discipline focus on an incorrect and misleading goal: "improving shareholder value". Much of this, of course, is a direct result of the financial frenzies of the past twenty years. We must acknowledge the interests of those who invest their funds in an organization, as stockholders. As their investments are easy to measure, through the market when stocks are publicly traded, we can easily be deluded into thinking that shareholder value is the be-all and end-all. Yet consider all the others who have similarly invested in the organization and whose "investments" are more difficult to measure. Employees invest their time and energy, both of which are far less liquid that the traded stocks of the shareholder. Suppliers invest their commitment and energy to the future of the organization, and often a high percentage of their sales come from a single customer. Customers, too, invest interest, money, and commitment to an organization. And there are other investors, such as communities in which an organization operates facilities, creditors who lend funds, the environment (air, water and land) affected by the organization, and regulators who represent the interests of society at large. Each of these have "investments" whose sum total is represented by the reputation of the organization, not its assets and earnings statement. The "value" of any organization lies in the confidence of each of these stakeholder groups in its future viability. Can it continue to deliver valued goods and services to its constituent base? That is the key question, not "what is the stock price today?"

So the correct goal of risk management is the creation and maintenance of stakeholder value in the organization.

While we continue to experience problems in the definition of risk, in understanding the broad nature of risk management itself, and in setting a correct goal, we have at least started to reach a consensus on the elements of an internal process.

That process has two simple steps: risk analysis and risk response. The first encompasses the identification of events that may affect our expected outcomes, their assessment in terms of likelihood, consequences, timing and public perceptions, and their analysis relative to organizational objectives. The second covers the controls to balance risk, trying to enhance favorable and reducing unfavorable outcomes, measuring and monitoring performance, and, perhaps most importantly, communicating risks and results to stakeholders.

Public discussion of risk management has evolved from articles in periodicals and books to the creation of national and international standards. The International Standards Organization developed a glossary of basic risk management terminology in an attempt to bring some cohesion to an erratic field. Other Standards organizations in Australia, New Zealand, Japan, Canada, Norway, and the United Kingdom now offer working risk management standards for their jurisdictions. New regulations from stock exchanges and governments address risk and response as critical issues for governing boards. From all these efforts comes a growing consensus on the key steps for building an effective process within any profit-making, nonprofit or governmental organization.

- *Board and senior management commitment* The process begins at the top, and includes reporting to and oversight by a responsible governing board.

- *Broad view of risk encompassing both reward and penalty* This brings risk management to the strategic level.
- *Common framework for the integrated analysis of all risks* This framework has yet to be achieved, although many are trying. Mixing credit, market, and operational risks to produce a single risk estimate is proving to be an elusive goal.
- *Single independent leader or coordinator for the process* The emergence of the Chief Risk Officer proves the value of a focal point for an organization-wide effort of building risk awareness.
- *Bottom-up risk assessments, continuing periodically* The best initial risk assessments always begin with the opinions of operating staff, supporting by guidance from specialists.
- *Necessity for clear and timely data* Ample and credible data exist for some risks, notably credit and some market areas, but they are seriously deficient for many operational risks.
- *Two-way communication with key stakeholders* Finally, the entire process of risk analysis and risk response should be shared with key stakeholder groups, as they are the organization's "investors." This involves both listening and telling!

As we move toward a fresh understanding of the nature of risk, of the strategic involvement of risk management itself, of the broad goal of the discipline and of the process required to generate results, there are three additional objectives that help clarify what we are trying to do. Each mandates a change in course for many organizations.

The first is *credibility*. If stakeholder confidence in the future is the goal, every step in risk analysis and risk response must be directed to enhancing credibility. It has been severely eroded by the events of the past few years, for all forms of organization. It begins with speaking the truth to stakeholders and the public, however embarrassing and damaging that truth may be. It also includes accepting responsibility for things that go wrong where the organization is responsible. External laws and regulations such as Sarbanes-Oxley in the US can never replace a responsible and responsive internal culture of risk awareness.

The second is *resilience*. No program of risk management, however sophisticated and broad, will ever identify all of an organization's possible unexpected events. Therefore building flexibility into the structure is a critical objective. Our organizations are always vulnerable to the unexpected. Can they become prepared? Can they react and survive? Can they actually take advantage of unusual events and turn them into enhanced stakeholder confidence?

The third course change is *perspective*. We no longer live in a world where short-term results are the only criteria. We need to restore the idea of the long view and change organizational cultures accordingly. This means gaining the acceptance and support of stakeholders as well.

Risk management continues to be a growing and evolving discipline, one that offers the promise to all organizations that we can live with uncertain futures more intelligently and responsibly.

CHAPTER 14

Does Risk Matter?

In 1998 and 2001 I wrote short articles for earthMatters *(Columbia University) and* Risk Management *(Risk & Insurance Management Society), respectively.*

> The remarkable fact that a great deal about nature can be extracted from a few facts and close reasoning.
>
> **Richard P. Feynman, *Six Easy Pieces,* Helix Books, Reading, MA 1994**

Does Risk Matter?

"Risk management" is cast as the new magic wand that promises greater chances for survival on "life's uncertain voyage," in Shakespeare's apt phrase. Recent financial fiascoes, from Barings to Orange County, are attributed to risk management weaknesses. Bill Ruckelshaus introduced the idea to the Environmental Protection Agency and today we have the Thompson-Levin bill in Congress that mandates rigorous risk-benefit analyses for all government regulations. Natural disasters—floods, windstorms, landslides and earthquakes—are subject to international forecasts and risk management attention, including the just-completed Internet symposium of the United Nations International Decade for Natural Disaster Recover (IDNDR). And author Peter Bernstein describes, in his best-selling *Against the Gods,* how we reached this point where we think that we can not only measure risk, but also manage it.

But what is risk management? Is it a replacement for the religious faith of the past that explained the unexplainable? Can it deliver a world in which we can live with uncertainty more prudently and responsibly? I define risk as "the possibility of deviation from the expected." Through education, experience and our genetic engineering, we create our own expectations of the future. The chance that it varies markedly from our expectations, favorably or unfavorably, is risk. In the Middle Ages and before, all divergences were attributable to the will of one god or another, and religious faith was the often so fatalistic that it discouraged change and encouraged the status quo. The growing sophistication of mathematics allowed us to begin a quantitative measurement of risk and fostered a new belief that we could construct a more reliable future, increasing the positive and reducing the negative outcomes.

Today, risk management, defined as "a discipline for living with uncertainty," is practiced to some degree in public policy, in major corporations, by the insurance industry, by safety, security and quality assurance adherents, and by contingency planners. It attempts to reduce to manageable limits the uncertainty that still circumscribes life despite our best efforts at forecasting and control. It holds promise for more effective use and protection of resources. I offer, however, three cautions.

The first is excessive risk aversion. Too often we define risk in its negative or pejorative sense. What can go wrong? How much can we lose? We become almost obsessive trying to eliminate any chance of loss. In so doing we overlook the positive side of every risk decision. We accept risk because we believe that the potential for a reward will more than offset any potential harm. Denying the existence of reward leads to a life-stultifying response of avoiding every risk. It is the ostrich approach. Risk aversion may well be the riskiest behavior of all. It's time to re-create the relish of risk, even as we try to measure its parameters using all the modern available tools of technology and communication.

The second caution is that of confidence and perception, two factors that are more subjective than quantitative. Statistics tell us that risk is measured by multiplying the potential likelihood of an event or decision outcome by its potential consequence. It is relatively easy to assign numbers to these factors. This, however, is a mathematical over-simplification. It omits any evaluation of our confidence in our estimate. How sound are the data on which the assessment is made? What critical assumptions underlie it? Do we have some gut reservations about it? We must modify the assessment by our level of confidence. The "likelihood" times "consequence" equation also omits the power of the perception of others in the risk assessment. Experts and medical studies, for example, may tell us that the mathematical risk of health injury from the use of silicon breast implants is negligible, but if enormous numbers of women believe otherwise, for whatever reason, the risk, and its purported effects, are very real indeed. What is the real risk of a meltdown or other disaster from a nuclear power station? After the catastrophe of Chernobyl, and the near miss at Three Mile Island, the public in the United States has grown so wary of nuclear power that new facilities are at a standstill and older facilities are being decommissioned. Public fear, rational or irrational, drives the risk response. And it is such a perception to which organizations must respond if they are to survive. The softer estimates of overall confidence and public perception must become part of the overall risk assessment.

The third caution is the most serious. It is possible that unintended adverse consequences may follow the best-intentioned risk responses. Overcome by the supposed enormity of some problem, we rush to protect and preserve, ignoring secondary and tertiary effects that could be more serious than the original situation. A manufacturing facility is plagued by employee pilferage. The pressured security director padlocks all exits except the front entry, now supervised by a guard and inspections. The pilferage ceases, but at what cost? If a fire occurs, how many employees will die or be injured in their panic attempt to evacuate through a single door? We build dams and levees to control floodwaters and provide new recreational areas. This inadvertently exacerbates the flood risk elsewhere. It may also eliminate spawning grounds for fish, causing ripple effects throughout an ecostructure. We are just beginning to learn about the global effects of El Niño and La Niña. Chaos theory predicts that the beat of a single butterfly's wings in China could create storms in North America. For some scientists, the elimination of the use of DDT has created environmental and health problems far more serious than those resulting from its use. In the United States we have panicked over asbestos, removing it from schools and buildings, at greater cost to owners and risk of injury to employees and contractors than if it had been encapsulated. Repercussions from decisions reverberate throughout systems. Too often risk managers allow the enormity of the problem at hand to obscure their broader, long-term vision. The rule for physicians is "do no harm." The rule for risk managers should be "do the least harm." Risk management needs to take a longer and harder view of possible consequences before recommending remedial action

Wise and responsible risk management requires a broader view of all risks, their effects, both positive and negative, the probable reaction of other stakeholders, fair or unfair, and the possible down-line consequences, however remote. Only in this way will this discipline contribute beneficially to our future.

Most of us are so involved in the daily turmoil of risk management that it is hard to step back from our discipline to reconsider its basic elements and ambiguities. This paper came from a speech in London in October 2000, refined in a follow-up lecture at Temple University in April 2001, and, finally, published in Risk Management *in October 2001. Originally and incorrectly titled "Four Cubed," it has but twelve sections, not sixty-four, so it has been renamed. It expands on four hypotheses, four questions, and four cautions drawn from some thirty years of observation and practice.*

Four Times Three

Four Hypotheses

Using the scientific approach, I raise four working hypotheses for the purpose of intensive discussion.

Risks cannot be segregated; they interact and affect one another. Take credit risk. We extrapolate from past experience and current and projected economic conditions to predict an expected level of credit losses. If they're substantially less than predicted, public expectations rise and new market risk is created. If credit losses exceed predictions, they create new operational risks if some managers succumb to fraud to hide disappointing results. If we respond to the risk of increased employee pilferage with more stringent security, such as reduced egress from facilities, we can increase the possibility of employee injury following a fire or similar disaster. Product and personnel losses inevitably lead to new regulatory restrictions. Risk resembles a woven garment: it is difficult to separate the yarns, and if we do, the result is a useless *mélange*. We lose the cohesive whole, since warp and woof create both beauty and utility. The goal is not to separate the yarns but to understand their interaction.

The Basel Committee of the Bank for International Settlements recognizes this interaction. The new Basel Capital Accords designate minimum capital requirements for managing credit, market and operational risks in financial institutions. The three risk areas are treated interactively. Our problem is that few of the current risk management sub-disciplines accept this hypothesis of inter-connection. Too many continue to address risks separately rather than as a part of the whole.

We must simplify our description of risks to understand them. It is essential to communicate to stakeholders our understanding of risks, their interactions, and our planned responses. When we obfuscate definitions with jargon, abstruse math, and convoluted prose, we lose the audience we must reach. For example, let's simplify the definition of risk to "a measure of the probability of deviation from the expected." Compare that to the prevailing monsters that run on for several sentences if not paragraphs! And how much of our audience comprehends deltas, gammas, thetas, and vegas, all part of the language of financial risk management? What about "parametizing the vol surface" and using the factor of "smile," terms heard at the recent GARP (Global Association of Risk Professionals) Conference in New York? It's time to simplify for better comprehension.

Communication is the weakest link in the risk management process and is generally omitted from process descriptions. Few organizations take the time to reduce what they know—and what they do not know—about risk, its organizational implications, and its responses into terms understandable to stakeholders. How many annual reports include a detailed description of risks and responses? How many organizations actively engage in two-way risk dialogues with groups of employees, customers, suppliers, members of the community, lenders, regulators, etc.? Too often risks and their management are buried in arcane terms, understandable only to the cognoscenti. Too often communication is limited to a few senior managers.

Risks cannot be transferred, only shared. Every organizational decision involves uncertainty. Some of these uncertainties are measurable and they are what we call "risk." How we've learned to improve our measurement is described in Peter Bernstein's seminal book, *Against the Gods.* We then manage the organization, accepting both uncertainties and risks and applying the best available responses.

We can share some portion of financial outcomes with others, such as investors (who take risk, plus and minus, through their stock purchases), lenders (who take it through loans), and insurers (through insurance). Yet neither one medium, nor all combined, can accept all risk. The residual parts, some of which are difficult to quantify, including reputation damage, political turmoil, and regulatory changes, remain with the decision-maker. Consider also that the act of sharing some risk creates a new risk—that of the inability of the counter-party to perform as expected. The idea of "transfer" creates a dangerous misimpression.

The risk management process can be described in two simple steps: risk analysis and risk response. All other steps in the process are sub-parts of these two. There is both beauty and comprehension in brevity. Within risk analysis lie risk identification, measurement, and assessment. Within response lie control, sharing, and communication. Too many textbooks, academics, and practitioners needlessly complicate the process, reducing comprehension. Risk management is a "discipline for dealing with uncertainty." Why add more?

Four Questions

Moving from my four hypotheses, I raise four questions to test these ideas and their application in the marketplace.

Is a risk manager a "policeman" or a "value-added provider?" Too many managers play the role of policeman, forever cautioning, "you can't do that," therefore setting limits on innovative activity. Operating managers generally see internal auditors and insurance managers in this role. I remember an insurance manager who tried to prohibit his company from using a hot air balloon for advertising purposes because, in his words, "it isn't covered by our insurance!" Or consider the auditor who challenges a new idea because it goes beyond current control capabilities. The shift to adding real value comes when the risk manager asks: "If there is potential reward in this activity, how can I help you do it more prudently and intelligently, avoiding unnecessary adverse results and accentuating favorable results?" To paraphrase Gilbert and Sullivan, the policeman's lot is not a happy one.

Which is more efficient and beneficial, addressing risks on an integrated basis or addressing them within demonstrated specialties? Integrating responses to all organizational risks is the underlying thesis of so-called enterprise, holistic, business, general, total, or strategic risk management. We experience resistance from traders, auditors, insurance buyers, safety managers, IT managers, security specialists and contingency planners, many of which believe that this approach challenges their unique "territory." That's only natural. We manage organizations as a whole. We should manage risks the same way. Consider my first hypothesis about the interactivity of risks. This does not mean that an all-powerful Czar rules the roost. What we need is someone to encourage the specialists to work with their counterparts and to coordinate their efforts. This move toward a more integrated approach to risk management is inevitable and appropriate. It is the only efficient approach.

What are the ultimate corporate goals, and should risk management be aligned with them? "Yes, obviously," you answer. Yet what if the organization has inadequate or deficient goals? For example, the goal of "Enhancing shareholder value" is too limited. If risk management aligns itself with such goals, difficulties are inevitable. What are responsible goals in today's world? AEP, the Virginia-based multi-national utility, has established four that are, in my mind, clear, simple, and far-sighted. They are: "Fairness, Integrity, Social Responsibility, and Fun." Fairness involves a "fair" return for all stakeholders, including shareholders, who invest their resources and time in the organization. Integrity demands the highest standards of personal and organizational honesty, something sadly lacking in many companies. Social Responsibility acknowledges the larger community, national and global context in which we operate. The last, Fun, is too often overlooked by most business leaders. Enjoy what you are doing! As Tom Peters noted, the most successful companies demonstrate a "love of product." Their stakeholders enjoy what they do. Yes, risk management should align itself with organizational goals, but managers should press for better goals if they are deficient. Don't be corporate doormats! Any organization-wide review of risks and responses begins with a proactive and fresh consideration of goals.

Should a risk manager be a follower or a leader? No matter where a "manager" resides in the organizational hierarchy, leadership is required. An insurance manager, quality control specialist, safety director or derivatives trader must, out of necessity, follow the lead of more senior officers, but that does not eliminate the need for independent thinking. Some years ago, I suggested that any self-respecting insurance risk manager should put his or her job on the line at least once a year in support of a new idea. While it was easy for me as a consultant to offer this counsel, the best managers actually did it.

What about the new interest in a "Chief Risk Officer?" A CRO is a leader and a coordinator who reports to both the CEO and the Board. Found primarily in financial institutions, the position is growing in utilities, energy companies and other non-financial organizations. I estimate that there are about 200 worldwide. Leadership involves the *courage* to challenge existing policies and practices and the *authority* to command an audience for the challenge. Many of the corporate debacles of the past thirty years have been the result of no one telling management that the Emperor has no clothes! The CRO, having access to both board and senior management, brings new leadership authority and organizational recognition to the risk management discipline.

Four Cautions

My four questions should test my four hypotheses. I now raise four cautions that surround the discipline of risk management.

Risk always involves tradeoffs and moral ambiguities. Aileen Kelly called this "the permanent possibility of moral uncertainty," in her introduction to Isaiah Berlin's *Russian Thinkers*. We carefully identify the measurable risk within the surrounding cloud of uncertainty. We use sophisticated qualitative and quantitative measurement devices, assess the favorable and unfavorable likelihood and consequences, and construct intelligent responses. Yet no matter what courses of action we take, our decisions involve tradeoffs. Costs offset anticipated benefits. If we create a new vaccine that protects millions from the ravages of a dread disease, we know there will some inevitable injuries or deaths. The automobile air bag saves lives but can also kill. The tradeoff lies in the benefit to many compared to the few losses. Morally, we do not want to cause any injury or death, but some will follow. Risk management teaches us to accept accountability and responsibility for *both* benefits and harms.

Accept the inevitability of unintended consequences. Recognize the limits of our knowledge. Every decision, no matter how carefully thought-out and studied by the experts, creates consequences that are impossible to anticipate. We prepare for them in risk management planning. As Peter Bernstein says, "The Law of Unintended Consequences can tell us a lot more about the future that we can learn from the Law of Large Numbers and other laws of that ilk." A classic example is the result of responses to our annual carnage on the highways. We built safer roads and collision-resistant cars. We mandated safety harnesses and air bags. The result: we now drive faster than ever before, instinctively compensating for these safety devices. Twenty years ago, 55 mph was the norm. Today it is 75!

Most observers believe that the guidelines of the Basel Committee Capital Accord, requiring minimum capital for credit, market and operational risks, plus stronger regulatory supervision and greater disclosure, increase the stability of the international banking system. Yet Avinash Persaud, of State Street Bank, in London, argues that regulators thereby promote "herding" and a greater chance of systemic failure because of the requirement for increased disclosure of bank positions. The result is lemming-like behavior in crises. Persaud suggests that "banks or investors like to buy what others are buying, sell what others are selling, and own what others own," since "they are more likely to be sacked for being wrong and alone than (for) being wrong and in company."

Unintended consequences can also be favorable. The effort spent on the Y2K bug, one that did not materialize as expected, cost us billions. Yet a recent study by the Maxwell School at Syracuse University argues that the "spillover effect" of Y2K expenditures materially improved the efficiency of information technology systems and their potential resistance to other future disruption.

Thalidomide is another example. First touted as an anti-bacterial agent, it caused monstrous birth defects in newborn babies and was quickly yanked from the market. Yet interest in the drug continued and today it is back in use, selectively, in successful treatment of leprosy and Kaposi's sarcoma.

Howard Kunreuther, of the University of Pennsylvania, and Paul Slovic, of the University of Oregon, wrote about macro-unintended consequences in 1999: ". . . we live in a world in which information, acting in concert with the vagaries of human perception and cognition, has reduced our vulnerability to pandemics of disease at the cost of increasing our vulnerability to massive social and economic catastrophes."

My point is that we can never know what will happen. Risk managers should stimulate serious conjecture about both the primary consequences of a decision and its possible secondary and tertiary effects. The expanding ripples are often more important than the initial splash.

Prepare for contingencies but continue to expect surprises. A corollary of the last comment, this caution asserts that contingency plans must be capable of responding to the totally unexpected as well as to the predictable.

Relish surprise! Risk is opportunity, bringing possible benefits and harms. Life is exploration and adventure. Never avoid risk. Too many practitioners approach risk as something to be mitigated or eliminated. This is a recipe for disaster. The goal is to understand risk intelligently and then manage our organizations in accord with that intelligence. As John Adams concluded in his book *Risk,* "Risks are constantly being transformed by our effort on the world and its efforts on us."

Conclusion

My four hypotheses, questions and cautions should create more curiosity than agreement. That is as it should be. If this occurs, we will move closer to the real goal of all risk management, that of enhancing the confidence of all stakeholders in the future of the organization. It's a discipline that is ready for adoption into both the culture and the strategy of most organizations.

If we fail to use this discipline creatively, risk management may become, in the words of J. W. Hackett's haiku:

A quiet crossroads . . .
On the door of an empty store
"Opportunity Shop"

CHAPTER 15

Risk Management and Monty Python

In 2005, the Institute of Risk Management in London, of which I have been a Fellow and member for many years, generously asked me to give its Annual Lecture. I took this as an opportunity to challenge several serious problems, including the perpetuation of conflicts of interest that destroy trust and confidence, the inability of different sub-disciplines of risk management to talk with one another, and the continuation of the idea that risk is something to be avoided. I gave the lecture in London on October 10, 2005. About two-thirds through, however, I experienced a complete blackout (a case of the fantods?) and could not continue. As I had just finished chastising the insurance brokerage business for its failure to change, a few in the audience thought that I had been struck by a thunderbolt from the gods of the brokers. Not so. Nor was the blackout an "intimation of mortality," paraphrasing Wordsworth, as the medics gave me a clean bill of health. It was merely the result of too little food, a bit of jet lag, and a warmer than usual auditorium. I recovered quickly and was able to meet my remaining obligations in London, with profound thanks to the staff and directors of the IRM and Willis, the firm that provided the venue.

> Writing, however, is a solitary pursuit, as monotonous as psychoanalysis though more lonely because you don't even get to see the patients. So it is easy in your own lighthouse keeper's isolation, to be taken in by your own propaganda and begin to believe the myth that you yourself have created.
>
> **Alfred Alvarez, *The Writer's Voice*, W. W. Norton & Co., New York 2005**

My comments in this year's IRM Lecture will be deliberately irreverent but masked with a bit of humor. They are irreverent for several reasons. First, this has been a calamitous year. We've been shocked by five disasters, four natural—the Indonesian tsunami, Hurricanes Katrina and Rita, and the South Asia earthquake—plus one thoroughly unnatural, the London bombings. Each of them remind us of the importance of trying to anticipate in some intelligent way the probable likelihood and possible consequences of unexpected events and of being prepared for the necessary short and long-term responses. Sadly, in all these cases we were unprepared. Too often we anticipate only those events that appear in databanks, not the outliers that appear to be remote contingencies. Yet these outliers are the most disruptive to our lives. Our apparent inability to prepare people for these events and the difficulty of restoring balance afterwards provokes some anger plus numerous irreverent thoughts.

Second, I believe I am permitted to express some disrespect because I am descended from two generations of preachers. My grandfather, the oldest of eleven children, became an Episcopal (Anglican) minister, serving in parishes in Virginia, Maine, North Dakota, Maryland and North Carolina. My father, also an Episcopal minister with parishes in New York, Philadelphia and Washington, was ordained in St. Paul's Cathedral here in London while studying tropical medicine preparatory to serving as a missionary in Liberia for three years. With all that reverent and multinational background I claim a right to express some occasional irreverence, especially to this audience in London.

I add humor to my observations as I've found that a direct frontal attack full of righteous indignation only rouses an equally self-righteous response. If I include a few notes of disarming humor, perhaps I can seduce others to remember, even consider my ideas. So, combining humor and my ecclesiastical background, this morning I plan to use as my lesson plan the Gospel According to Monty Python.

I have some serious concerns about our evolving and continuously intriguing discipline. *My first concern is the proper focus of risk management.* I maintain the primary goal *must* be that of building and maintaining *trust*, the confidence that various stakeholders have in any organization, be it governmental, nonprofit or corporate. We spend far too much time and energy thinking about costs, or profits, or shareholders, and thereby dilute our effectiveness even as we satisfy the number crunchers. Trust is in especially short supply in the area of financial services in which blatant and continued conflicts of interest have eroded the very condition essential to this marketplace. I intend to focus on these conflicts this morning because our trust in each other is minimal and because those outside financial services have even more jaundiced views. Their perception is the reality that we face.

What, then, can the Gospel of Monty Python tell us about this first issue? A great deal, I find.

I trust most of you remember the lesson in these scriptures about the dead parrot. In it a customer played by John Cleese enters a pet shop holding a dead parrot in a cage, complaining that the bird, purchased only a half-hour earlier, is dead. The shop owner, played by Michael Palin, suggests that the creature is simply "resting," or "stunned," or "pining for the fjords", as it is, of course, a Norwegian bird. Cleese responds that the only reason that it is upright on its perch is because it was nailed there.

Let's reconsider this lesson in light of the recent disclosures of the Attorney General of the State of New York, Eliot Spitzer. Mr. Spitzer now plays the role of the angry buyer and the head of a large insurance brokerage firm plays the shop owner. Spitzer holds not a parrot but the business model of the insurance industry, the model that is riddled with inappropriate payments, conflicts of interest, bid rigging and other devious machinations. Huddled in the background, peeking around a door leading to the backroom are the worried faces of the leaders of the larger brokers and insurers.

Spitzer: Look, my lad, I've had just about enough of this. That business model is definitely deceased. When I bought it a while ago, you assured me that its lack of movement was due to the fact that it's been in use for more than fifty years.

Broker #1: It's probably pining for the good old days.

Spitzer: Pining for the good old days, what kind of talk is that? Why did it fall flat on its back the minute that I looked at it?

Broker #1: The insurance business model prefers quiet, no attention, and above all no questions from either customers or regulators.

Spitzer: The only reason that this business model is sitting on its perch is that you brokers and insurers nailed it there and hid the hammer from your customers.

Broker #1: But the customers haven't complained in fifty years.

Spitzer: That's because you co-opted them. This business model has passed on. It is no more. It has ceased to be. It's expired and gone to meet its maker. This is a late business model. It's a stiff. Bereft of life, it rests in peace. It you hadn't nailed it up, it would be pushing up the daisies. It's rung down the curtain and joined the choir invisible. This is an ex-business model.

Broker # 1: Well, I'd better replace it then. (He turns to his friends in the back office and they discuss the problem. They boot two CEOs out the back door, and Broker Head # 2 returns to face Mr. Spitzer.)

Broker # 2: Here's our brand new business model, with no contingent commissions, at least for a few of us, but we will still accept fees from insurance companies to compensate us for all the work we do for them, and reinsurance commissions, and interest income of fiduciary funds. This new model is called a slug.

Spitzer leaves in exasperation to run for governor.

Parenthetically I acknowledge that we gather in this room this morning through the generosity of a broking house that I have just subjected to a bit of ridicule and humor. I am properly grateful to that firm but it doesn't alter the circumstances that I describe.

That's what we face this October in London: a refurbished business model hurriedly put together by the brokers and insurers, one that is no change at all. It is a slug! Individual brokers are going to jail for bid rigging (nine more from Marsh were indicted just three weeks ago), but the larger firms avoid retribution by firing some staff, paying pay enormous fines, now over $1 billion, and avoiding any admission of guilt. They dump a few CEOs for effect. But no one acknowledges that the system is broken; no one is honest enough to say that it's time for a new model. Everyone, including I am sad to say, the majority of their customers, tries to paper over the adverse publicity and return to a semblance of the old system. The buyers' associations are equally complicit. Witness what the executive director of the Risk & Insurance Management Society (RIMS) said last year: "Our members appreciate what the broker is doing. They don't care where the payments are coming from so long as they are disclosed." That's like saying, "I don't care how you rip me off; just tell me how you are doing it!" Or like Oliver Twist saying, "Please, sir, will you take some more from me." What else can RIMS say when the majority of its operating income comes its annual trade show, heavily supported by payments and contributions from the many vendors, brokers being foremost. AIRMIC (UK's counterpart to RIMS) is hardly blameless: undeterred by all this adverse publicity, it proudly announced this spring a £400,000 "partnership agreement" with three brokers and seven insurers, most of which are involved in the Attorney General's complaints, to support "new research and services." These are the same organizations that have been steadily bilking AIRMIC's members. It is time to draw the line on these sponsorships and relationships. Yet so long as the customers don't complain, how can we expect these organizations to help eliminate the conflicts and habits condoned if not encouraged for so many years?

The problem of conflict of interest is "running rampant" in financial services (words from *The Economist*). Accounting firms sell patently illegal tax shelters. Mutual funds permit late trading by favored stockbrokers. Pension consultants take payments from the investment firms they recommend. Stockbrokers slant their research in favor of their large investment clients. A hedge fund pays a commission to a so-called "independent" advisory firm. And, of course, insurance brokers profess to serve their clients and yet take all manner of behind-the-scene contingent commissions, gratuities, reinsurance commissions, fees for "services" to insurers, interest income on fiduciary funds, and low-interest loans, plus owning or holding substantial interests in insurers and reinsurers. And all of this is in addition to the up-front commissions from these same insurers, payments that are and have been for more than fifty years a blatant compromise of their required integrity to customers. We've corrupted a system that mandates trust between client and advisor and "utmost good faith" between buyer and insurer! David Shirreff commented on this development in his book, *Dealing With Financial Risk* (*The Economist*/Profile Books, Ltd., London 2004): "The standards that crept in during the 1990s condoned rapacity on behalf of bankers and their institutions and rewarded it, whereas scruples about the client's best interests were seen as squeamish and weak."

It's time to stop being squeamish and weak!

I have no objection to any or all of these payments from insurers so long as the insurance intermediary correctly and honestly states that it is an "agent" of the insurer, a sales representative, and a hawker of coverage, not an objective representative of the client. Then the buyer can properly beware sales pitches and twists. But to swallow the idea that these multiple payments do not, in fact, alter the objectivity of the placing broker is to accept the idea that the dead parrot is actually alive and well. They lead inevitably to corrupt behavior on the part of some brokers. In a recent paper entitled "The Economics of Insurance Intermediaries," David Cummins and Neil Doherty of the Wharton School at the University of Pennsylvania, conclude that contingency commissions may actually help all parties to the insurance transaction. But they also suggest that the "role of the intermediary should be aligned with that of the insurer." If that is true, the there is no such thing as a broker, only an agent. I grant that insurers always will have a problem with "adverse selection," one that the proximity of the broker to the customer can help alleviate, but reformatting the underwriting process to permit a much closer connection between underwriter and buyer will help the situation far more than outrageous incentive compensation to brokers. Note that the American Insurance Association actually commissioned the Cummins-Doherty paper, something that calls into question its objectivity, and that the magazine of the US insurance sales community, *Leading Edge,* promptly jumped on it as a justification for *all* contingent commissions! If contingent commissions can be misused, and they are by some, then how and when can a buyer trust a broker? Then what about the basic commission system? Won't it be misused as well? Continuation of *all* commissions is unacceptable, and disclosure is a sham.

The problem is not that the *buyers* don't know what is going on. They know but they don't seem to care. That's the sad part of our story. They are therefore complicit in supporting this system of conflicts by not raising the hue and cry for change. They've sat quietly on their hands and wallets, stuffed with the goodies handed out by brokers (theatre tickets, vacations, fancy dinners, lavish hospitality suites at annual conventions). Over the years, many of us on the periphery of this business have complained vociferously: I registered my first complaint in 1971 and have repeated it almost every year thereafter, but the force of cash and convention overwhelmed our few voices.

What is the solution? RIMS and several other organizations argue for simple disclosure, as if we are naïve enough to believe that any brokerage firm will willingly set forth on paper all the possible perks received from insurers. Even with full disclosure, the temptation remains to steer business to the insurer with the fattest perks, the highest commissions. A more radical change is necessary, one that AIRMIC and its members support. I argue that we must substitute client fees for *all* commissions, so that fees are the *sole* source of income to a broker. This is the first and mandatory step in creating a new business model. A broker should agree with its client to accept only fee income directly negotiated and paid by the client. I do acknowledge that there will still be brokers who try and take payments behind the scenes: a fee system is not an ultimate panacea, but it is, I believe, the critical first step. As Ronald Reagan famously said, "Trust but verify." AIRMIC, in contrast to its counterpart in the United States, has shown leadership on this issue. Now let's see who follows.

All of us—brokers, insurers, buyers, regulators, and commentators—have tolerated for far too long a system that creaks with conflicts, anachronisms, and inefficiencies. Much of this may not have been "illegal" in the strict sense of the law, but isn't it time we cleaned up the act? Change is the prevailing movement today in other financial services, as we change the way we work with stockbrokers, mutual funds, pension advisers, and accountants. It's time to dump the dead parrot of the insurance industry along with the slug proposed as its successor.

I've dwelt on this subject as an illustration of the proper goal of our discipline: re-creating a sense of trust and confidence in the working relationships with financial advisors as well as all stakeholders. Safety and environmental records, premium costs, governmental expenditures and net profits are important, but *trust* transcends them all as the goal. Only with trust and confidence in an organization can it present its perspectives and ideas to stakeholders with a real potential for acceptance and understanding.

I have two more serious concerns about our discipline.

My second concern is the growing fragmentation of risk management, as different practitioners define their narrow interests to the exclusion of others. Interdisciplinary dialogue and cooperation are critical to our future but few try to bridge the growing chasms that separate credit, market, operational, actuarial, audit, safety, insurance and public policy advocates. We are retreating to the very silos of selfishness that enterprise risk management is trying to undermine.

To illustrate it, I draw from another part of the Gospel According to Monty Python, the story about the Bruces. You remember it, I'm sure. The philosophy faculty of an Australian university gathers for a meeting. In spite of an enormous range of intellectual interests, from Socratic and Aristotelian to the theories of Kant, Hobbes and Hegel, these professors all share the same name, Bruce. Here's a modified and updated version of that discussion, where the heads of the major global risk management associations play the Bruces:

First Bruce: G'day mates!

Other Bruces: *(in unison)* Bon jour, ohayo, 'morning, guten tag, buenos dias!

Second Bruce: I'm glad to see we have some sheilas here today. (*He motions to the leaders of the Risk & Insurance Management Society, the Institute of Internal Auditors and the International Federation of Risk and Insurance Management Associations.)*

Third Bruce: Do we see any differences among strategic, enterprise, integrated, holistic, qualitative or quantitative risk management?

All Bruces: No, they're all Bruce to me!

Fourth Bruce: What about the SRA, IRM, RIMS, IFRIMA, IIA SOA, CAS, RMA, IOSH, GARP and PRMIA?

All Bruces: They're all Bruce to me!

Fifth Bruce: What about all these standards from New Zealand, Australia, Japan, UK, Canada, Norway, and COSO, and the Dey, Cadbury, and Hampel committees?

All Bruces: They're all Bruce to me!

First Bruce: Right, as we're all in agreement, crack tubes! (*Sound of cans of Foster's beer being opened simultaneously)*

Would that this serendipitous scene becomes reality! Unfortunately today I see a growing failure of interdisciplinary discourse. In the words of John Adams and Michael

Thompson, from a 2002 paper, this discourse ranges from "an unresponsive monologue" to a "shouting match amongst the totally deaf." Most members of the alphabet soup of associations I cited don't even know that the others exist. Over the past three years, when attending the annual meetings of these associations, I've often asked how many can even identify the other organizations. In every case the response is less than 10%! How can so many advocates of risk management be so ignorant of their fellow practitioners?

We must expand our knowledge of others who speak risk management. The oldest groups, including the Casualty Actuarial Society and the Risk Management Association (formerly Robert Morris Associates), go back to the early 1900s. The largest is the Institute of Internal Auditors, with 107,000 members worldwide, dwarfing both GARP (the Global Association of Risk Professionals) and PRMIA (the Professional Risk Managers' International Association), which claim over 20,000 members each. And if you don't think the internal auditors are a risk management group, just take time to study many of the risk management materials they have published. They are among the best and clearest to date. Age and size, of course, are not as important as influence, and here the Society of Risk Analysis, the smallest, probably exerts the greatest effect on governmental and public policies. That the topics of cost-benefit analyses and sophisticated risk assessments rank high in governmental work in the United States is directly attributable to an ex-President of the Society for Risk Analysis serving in the Office of Management and Budget.

What should we do? The first step is to acknowledge that each of these organizations plays an important role in the development of the discipline of risk management. Next, each organization should create an *ad hoc* liaison committee to stimulate contact and cooperation with other groups. Our own IRM leads in this effort, along with the IIA, in trying to bring these organizations closer together. Third, why not reach out to our fellow groups by having plenary interdisciplinary sessions at our regular annual conferences? The SOA, CAS, and PRMIA, did that last spring in Chicago, and RIMS is planning a similar interdisciplinary panel in Hawaii in 2006. Fourth, we students of risk management should subscribe to and read the publications of these other sub-disciplines. Nothing is better to help stimulate the ferment of new ideas. And fifth, we should invite our fellow students to attend our local meetings. As the Gospel says, we're all Bruces!

My final concern is that we continue to view risk itself too narrowly, focusing only on the downside consequences of unexpected events. In so doing we create a new and malicious form of risk aversion that in time will cripple innovation and creativity. This is the growing propensity for those involved with risk analysis and risk management to look only on the dark side of future events. It's a rather gloomy view from where I stand.

The financial risk managers, the quants and their allies, are so encumbered with the dictates of Basel 1 and 2 that their models for credit, market and operational risks are focused only on possible losses and the effect of these losses on regulatory capital requirements. As Avinash Persaud pointed out in his Gresham College lectures here in London a year ago, the growing bank aversion to risk may create a horde of lemmings, following each other instinctively for fear of being out of step with the herd. Perversely, this may actually increase systemic risk even as it reduces individual downside risk for each financial institution.

The internal auditors have now spent over a decade helping to create the mandates of COSO, whose recent paper on enterprise risk management is a perfect example of Babelian jargon, a work lacking clarity, cohesion and cogency. Their entire approach is to create new controls to prevent losses.

The safety engineers think only of reducing lost-time frequency and severity and justifying their importance within organizations. Similarly the security specialists want to protect both tangible and intangible property, such as information, from the depredations of hackers, thieves and an entire outside world bent on stealing us blind. The public policy gurus see nothing but disaster looming on the horizon: tsunamis, floods, hurricanes, typhoons, genetically-engineered foods run amok, electromagnetic injuries, asteroids, bio-terrorism, global warming and, worst of all, strangelets, one of which could run rampant and reduce the earth to a diameter of less than one hundred meters. The uniform response to all these fears is that remarkable golden rule of all the Luddites before them, do nothing for fear of some adverse outcome. This is known as the "Precautionary Principle," an idea that freezes creativity and innovation. Finally, of course, the insurance world sees risk only as a negative outcome It sits on its hands as the world economy expands, providing less and less coverage for the growing costs of unexpected events. Its role as a financer of risk, like the grin of the Cheshire Cat, seems to be diminishing annually into the haze, until it may finally disappear altogether.

Benjamin Hunt's *The Timid Corporation,* published in 2003, chronicles the effects of public policy, regulation, litigation, and human fears and, yes, even the tools of risk management, all of which force corporations into a "defensive mode." They dumb down innovation and avoid taking chances, in their obsession with preserving "shareholder value." They react too fearfully to the warnings of outsiders such as single-issue NGOs and create the fiasco of the Brent Spar decision of Royal Dutch/Shell. So we drift into tacit adoption of the precautionary principle, fearful of any change. The Rector of my boarding school issued a cogent warning over a decade ago. He argued that a leader who is too risk averse sends throughout an organization messages that affect every level of decision-making, causing lost opportunities. He concluded: we must avoid becoming creatures "afraid to risk what they have achieved for what they might achieve."

This mounting aversion to risk suggests, in the words of your own Prime Minister, in a paper he delivered to University College London on May 26, 2005 that "something is seriously awry." He went on, "We are in danger of having a wholly disproportionate attitude to the risks we should expect to run as a normal part of life." His attack on the growing "compensation culture" is warranted, especially as we in the United States have brought it to a high level of idiocy. Mr. Blair called for a "more sensible debate." I agree, and I believe this debate should start with an acknowledgement that risk itself, the measure of the probable likelihood and consequences of an unexpected event, includes both favorable and unfavorable outcomes. John Adams, of University College London, calls it correctly: "risk management is a balancing act involving uncertainty about rewards and costs."

He explicitly includes "rewards." Richard Posner agrees, in his magnificent analysis of potential disasters, *Catastrophe: Risk and Response* (Oxford University Press, Oxford 2005): "Risk aversion implies an asymmetrical attitude towards gains and losses." When we include only downside results in our definition of risk we inevitably slip towards risk aversion. The Prime Minister summed it up in May: "Government cannot eliminate all risk. A risk-averse scientific community is no scientific community at all. A risk-averse business culture is no business culture at all. A risk-averse public sector will stifle creativity and deny to many the opportunities to be creative while supplying a few with compensation payments . . . . Sometimes we have to accept (that) no-one is to blame."

The September 2005 series of *Financial Times* articles on "Mastering Risk" is a breath of fresh air. Eamonn Kelly and Steve Weber's opening piece on September 8 put risk in proper focus. We must return, they argue, to the original concept, born of "European seafaring adventurism," one that contains a "powerful sense of opportunity and reward as well as downside and danger." Our organizations require an entirely new attitude in dealing with internal, market and external environments. "When advantage lies mostly in the unknown and the uncertain, the ability to sense and learn faster, to correct mistakes and drop losing bets, to tolerate ambiguity and live with, even embrace, ambivalence, becomes absolutely essential." The authors conclude: "Loss aversion is not a way to win. Re-embrace risk as a source of advantage."

The aftermath of hurricanes Katrina and Rita, in which so many poor families were uprooted, prompted the right risk management response from Carlos Eire, a professor at Yale University. He wrote to them (*The New York Times,* Sept. 25, 2005): "Embrace your rage. It is utterly justified. Nature dealt you a low blow, and your government made it worse. Your city deserved to have better levees, and in the richest nation in the world, you could have easily had them. Your leaders failed you at every turn, especially if you were among the poor. But embrace your survival, too, along with all those surprising acts of kindness and all of the unexpected opportunities that came your way because of the disaster. Never forget that gain and loss are twins conjoined at the heart." His reminder is that opportunity is omnipresent with loss: all depends on how you look at risk.

I turn again to the Gospel of Monty Python for more light on this problem, finding it in that immortal film, *The Life of Brian.* At its conclusion, as Brian hangs crucified in Palestine, he and his fellow victims are encouraged to look on the bright side of life!

As the song goes:

> Cheer up, Brian. You know what they say.
> Some things in life are bad.
> They can really make you mad.
> Other things just make you swear and curse.
> When you're chewing on life's gristle,
> Don't grumble. Give a whistle.
> And this'll help turn things out for the best.
> And always look on the bright side of life.

If life seems jolly rotten,
There's something you've forgotten,
And that's to laugh and smile and dance and sing.
When you're feeling in the dumps,
Don't be silly chumps.
Just purse your lips and whistle. That's the thing.
And always look on the bright side of life.

So I reach the end of this morning's homily, one that combines a bit of irreverence and a touch of humor to remind us all of three critical ingredients of our discipline. I learned my method from my reverend antecedents. In any homily, first tell your congregation what you intend to say. Then say it. And, finally, remind them at the end what you just said. Here's my summation.

First, always work to build and maintain trust. Beware the dead parrot and its successor, the slug. *Second*, we are all named Bruce in our quest to develop risk management. Speak and listen to all your compatriots in the related sub-disciplines. And, *finally*, risk embodies both good and bad outcomes. Avoid risk aversion and "always look on the bright side of life."

Thank you for listening to my sermon.

CHAPTER 16

Introduction:
The Future of Risk Management, Again

I started this collection of essays with a "preliminary conclusion," a working hypothesis about the nature of risk and risk management. I've tested this hypothesis against many of my thoughts, as well as my fantods, from more than a decade ago to the present. So it is only natural to end with an "introduction," a summary of my ever-changing mind.

I find that "certainty" is a false idol. We delude ourselves if we think we can ever be "certain." Similarly the attempt to find "closure" after unexpected events is trite, selfish, and impossible. Trying to explain your way out of a mistake, hoping that everyone will forget, is exactly the wrong approach. Store that mistake, that unexpected event, in your memory bank. Then learn from the experience. Risk management is a combination of memory and conjecture. Beware tying up loose ends!

So I end by trying to start again!

> . . . caught unawares in the great, deep, and confusing eddy of contingency, which has other contingency streams running into it, some visible, some too deep-cruising for us to know about.
>
> **Richard Ford, "How Was It to be Dead?"**
> ***The New Yorker,* August 28, 2006**

Just a few hundred years ago, intelligent people believed that astrology could tell us the future and phrenology could predict human behavior. Both have slipped into mythology as we gained new knowledge. Could this happen to risk management, our latest exercise in prediction?

Periodically I try to look at the future development of our expanding discipline to guess what might occur. My first essay on this subject appeared in *Risk Management Reports* in January 1982, when I forecast it would become more decentralized, be led by a senior staff officer, and respond to global instead of local and national demands. I tried the crystal ball again in 1996 when I noted the growing "multidimensionality" (awkward word!) of risk responses and the need for a broader, cross-discipline approach. Most recently, I wrote "Risk Management: Past, Present and Future" in May 2003, citing credibility, resilience, and perspective as three future critical issues facing risk officers.

Now I'm at it again. In September 2006, I participated in a panel discussion on the future at the Risk & Insurance Management Society's Canadian conference in Calgary. The following comments are drawn from that session. I owe my fellow panelists, John Adams, Emeritus Professor of Geography at University College London, and Beaumont Vance, Senior Enterprise Risk Manager at Sun Microsystems in Denver (and now editor of *Risk Management Reports)*, for their stimulation for this latest peek into the future.

How far has risk management come and where is it today? Its evolution over the past 400 years is based on the scientific collection of information, the measurement of probabilities, the vagaries of decision theory, and the latest elements of behavioral economics. Today its composite pieces combine in the responsibilities of a Chief Risk Officer. But risk management remains fragmented. Different sub-disciplines persist in emphasizing their own particular skills and specialties (credit risk, market risk, internal auditing, safety & health, public policy, actuarial science, and insurance). It is dominated by responses to and controls for the mounting demands for better governance and compliance with new regulations (SOX and Basel II). It still cannot measure concrete benefits to an organization other than in loose and qualitative terms, and, perhaps most troubling, few organizations have undertaken serious two-way risk and response communications with their stakeholders.

Where is risk management going? Will it disappear or mutate, like other management fads, as Michael Power, of the London School of Economics, argues? Will it become a profession in its own right, like accountancy or the law? Will quantitative practitioners dominate the field? Or will it blend into and be absorbed by the mainstream of management thinking, in areas like strategic and contingency planning?

I don't know, but I can and will raise questions and conjectures to help us think more creatively about its development over the next quarter-century. One thing we *have* learned is that uncertainty remains the dominant feature of our lives. As the past and current Chairmen of the Federal Reserve Bank in Washington have persuaded us, only the foolish imagine that they can eliminate it. Risk management must begin by accepting the futility of predicting the future. At best we can suggest a range of possible changes, and too often even these are tempered by wishful thinking! Just extrapolating the past into the future—a bit more, a bit less or just the same—denies the probability of major diversions. The unusual and unexpected always happen. Progress comes from employing continuing doubt about what we do and how we do it, coupled with continuing curiosity about improving our lot.

This paper explores possible new goals, new standards, new understandings and new tools.

First, **new goals** Current risk management aims at relatively narrow and tactical objectives: saving money; reducing credit, market or operational losses; improving shareholder value. The approach to risk analysis is both too complex and fragmented. Risk responses are seldom linked to broader organizational problems and strategic issues, despite the prevailing lip service tendered to enterprise risk management.

To survive and play a constructive organizational role, risk management must adopt more ambitious goals.

1. The new primary goal must be to *build and maintain the confidence of critical stakeholder groups* in the organization. Trust and reputation, while difficult to measure, are an organization's principal assets. This means reaching out not only to shareholders, management and employees, but also to customers, suppliers, regulators, the communities where we operate, and the public at large. This also means trying to create "value" for *all* stakeholders. While I don't dismiss the legal responsibility of management to shareholders in a publicly-held company, my point is we are "responsible" to more than investors and there is more to "value" than stock prices.
2. Risk management must teach an organization how to cope not with risk that is measurable to some degree, but also with *the broader and persistent fog of uncertainty and doubt*. This means improving organizational resilience to the inevitable unexpected contingencies. The most sophisticated risk assessments can never measure all uncertainties. We must adapt to surprises.
3. Risk management must be *opportunistic*. Even in the throes of disaster, we should seek possible strategic advantage for our stakeholders. This means understanding that risk embodies both favorable as well as unfavorable unexpected outcomes. Risk management is a technique for improving our risk taking. This idea is hardly new. Jacques Bernouilli, one of the fathers of the art of probability, suggested the same theme in 1713, in his *Art of Conjecture.* Adam Gopnik confirmed this understanding in a recent article in *The New Yorker* ("Read It and Weep," August 28, 2006) when he wrote, "Terror makes fear, and fear stops thinking." If we look only at possible downside results, we create fear, and then we stop thinking rationally. We become risk averse, crippling initiative. Risk aversion leads to a narrowed focus, then self-assurance, and finally the absence of doubt and curiosity. This is the death knell for any organization.

Second, **new standards** Over the past fifteen years, we've developed a variety of local, national and global "standards," such as Basel I, COSO I, COSO II, and the Australian/New Zealand Risk Management Standard 4360, revised in 2004. Canada, the United Kingdom, Norway, and Japan have similar standards. Basel II is being prepared for adoption worldwide. Most efforts improve the breed, although the COSO II (Committee of Sponsoring Organizations) monster in the United States set us back several years. The Australian/New Zealand effort should be the bellwether, if risk management is to continue to evolve and flourish. Some fear "standards" as possible regulatory imperatives that could stifle initiative and innovation, preferring instead "guidelines." Call them what you will: they are stepping-stones to improvement.

These standard/guideline makers need the active input of representatives of all the sub-disciplines, as often their working committees are too parochial. Six current projects and developments will affect the future of risk management standards.

1. The Bank for International Settlements, in Basel, has been working for some years on *Basel II*, a voluntary set of guidelines for regulators and major banks around the world, with a goal of application by various national regulatory bodies in 2007 and 2008. In addition to upgrading approaches for credit and market risk analyses, Basel II now includes operational risks in setting minimum capital requirements. Most important is Pillar 3, mandating more disclosure and transparency. Some observers warn, however, that Basel II may have unintended consequences, such as reducing individual initiative and inducing lemming-like behavior that could *increase* systemic problems. (See www.bis.org)
2. The *International Organization for Standardization* (ISO), under the leadership of several managers instrumental in the Australian and New Zealand work, is now developing a new global "guideline" for risk management. Its Technical Committee hopes to complete a final working draft in 2008. Its goals are clarity, consensus and brevity, and, to date, progress is encouraging. This work will add to the earlier excellent ISO glossary of risk management terms. Those interested can go to its website (www.iso.org).
3. The *Royal Society* for the Encouragement of the Arts, Manufactures and Commerce (the RSA), in London (website: *www.thersa.org*) is embarked on a three-year Commission on Risk. As one of its objectives is to "embolden risk," I anticipate some challenging insights. Three ideas from the early materials of this commission confirm my anticipation:

   (a) "Risk is rarely given a balanced view."
   (b) "We cannot eliminate risk; we have to live with it."
   (c) "Enlightened risk taking should be the goal."

4. In January 2006, the *US Office of Management and Budget (OMB)* published a "Proposed Risk Assessment Bulletin," suggesting regulatory "standards" for safety, health, and environmental agencies. The OMB hopes these standards will reduce the cost of regulation and speed compliance. But, according to some critics, they may instead delay prompt action on dangerous materials and practices and, as well, cost taxpayers more.
5. A more ominous development is the growing global application of the *"precautionary principle"* to governance and the regulation of new ideas and technology. Simply stated, this "principle" argues that, if the possible negative

results of a new idea, technique or technology are difficult to determine, government should suspend or stop it. This principle is contrary to sound risk management. Unexpected consequences, both favorable and unfavorable, are always a part of progress, but increased adoption of the "precautionary principle" could cripple innovation and creativity.

6. Another form of standardization is the use of risk management "*certifications*." Do we really have to continue this mania of attaching initials after one's name to confer status? Do they mean the recipient is inherently more intelligent and a better manager? I doubt it. Compare the certifications that abound in the risk management arena, from such organizations as RIMS, National Alliance for Insurance Education and Research (CRM), the Insurance Institute of America (its ARM designation dates to 1965), GARP (FRM), RMA, PRMIA (PRM), Institute for Risk Management, and Institute of Internal Auditors. Now ERMII (Enterprise Risk Management Institute International Ltd.) proposes yet another one. GARP and PRMIA, however, promise to eclipse all others (their exams are financial and tough!). GARP's FRM (Financial Risk Manager) and PRMIA's PRM now count over 9,000 holders and more than 7,000 exam takers in 2006. Given the expansion of job openings in financial risk management, is there any doubt that these two certifications will be the global standards in the next decade, simply by the weight of numbers? Employers will dictate which initials carry the most market weight.

I have two nagging questions. First, is our future therefore in the hands of the quants? Second, do these written "standards" and "certifications" really improve our ability to manage uncertainty or are they in fact regressions that inhibit experimentation and new ideas?

Third, **new understandings** We should challenge some of the prevailing understandings of what we do, including the ideas that risk is bad, that we should avoid risk, and that risks are separate, each to be approached tactically and with its own solutions.

New understandings will likely evolve in the next decade. One may be the idea that we should enhance *risk taking*. To do so we will learn how to make *simultaneous analyses* of both unexpected upside and downside results. Risks will be addressed *strategically*, even if we continue to use separate tactics for some of them. We *cannot* predict the future; we can only suggest possible scenarios (uncertainty and ambiguity are always with us). And, foremost, risk management will become an *essential part of contingency planning* and perhaps be subsumed by it.

Much of the future depends on how we interpret risk itself. Jack Dowie suggested in 1999 that we dispense with the word entirely, as it is already so misinterpreted that it creates instant confusion. Stevyn Gibson, in 2005, correctly noted that "risk has a dual nature" in terms of its perception by different parties and its objective reality as determined by "experts." (See *Risk Management: An International Journal,* Vol. 7, No. 4). John Adams, one of my co-panelists, expands this thought into three types of risk.

The first is *"directly perceived"* using a combination of instinct, intuition and experience. It includes much of operational risk and is therefore managed by judgment.

The second is *"risk perceived through science,"* the "realm of quantified risk assessment," employing the skills of the market trader, credit analyst, and actuary. Econometric models are the flavor of the day. Adams notes that while this area of risk assessment now dominates risk literature, it may not in the future, as many of these quantitative measures "rest ultimately on subjective assumptions."

The third is that of *"virtual risk."* "When science cannot settle an argument, people feel liberated to argue from their pre-established convictions, beliefs, prejudices and superstitions." As Adams says, "we are thrown back on judgment." And so, he concludes, risk management is always a "balancing act."

Fourth, **new tools** Most observers agree that we need and will develop new and sophisticated tools and technology to spur our understanding of uncertainty. Crouhy, Galai and Mark, in their latest textbook, *Essentials of Risk Management* (McGraw-Hill, New York 2006), suggest that "today, ERM largely exists in name only." I agree. They offer ten possible future extensions, and two are pertinent to this discussion. The first is that "risk transparency" will be expected and even mandated. Stakeholders want, and will get, more disclosure. Telling the world about your risks will be awkward, even painful in many instances, but it *is* the future. Second, we will develop new risk transfer (I prefer the words risk sharing) mechanisms to improve and spread risks globally. Just as credit derivatives have swamped all other forms of credit risk sharing, including traditional insurance, many other risks may be pooled and securitized. This is a part of the continuing search for more efficient and reliable contingency funding. Pooling among organizations and with government and multi-national groups will be more common.

Beaumont Vance, another co-panelist in Calgary, has an intriguing forecast. Just as today's stock market analysts use a Bloomberg machine to access minute-to-minute data about trading conditions, tomorrow risk analysts will have access to overall "risk assessments" of individual organizations and even governments, assessments that change instantly whenever internal or external conditions warrant. In today's insurance world, we make risk-financing changes *annually.* In the financial world we obtain *daily* changes to VaR. In the future we'll have *instant* risk assessment changes, altering financial arrangements, stock prices, risk responses, and especially stakeholder confidence. Development of a "Risk Bloomberg" machine is an intriguing idea, but would it be overly dependent on "measurable" as compared to the more qualitative risks? How can we input the subjective? Should we?

Here are several additional "tools" for future use:

- Measurement of an entire *portfolio* of risks and their effects on an organization. ERM proposes this idea but it remains in the future.
- Continuous re-evaluation of how risks are modified by the actions, responses and non-action of others. Risk assessments and responses never occur in a vacuum.

Leigh Buchanan and Andrew O'Connell ("A Brief History of Decision Making,") wrote a superb summary of what we have learned about risk, intuition, group decision-making, and "thinking machines" in the January 2006 issue of *Harvard Business Review.* We have much to learn about the process of decision making in rapidly changing conditions, where new information is instantaneous.

— Improved scenario analyses combining quantitative and *qualitative* assessments, leading to better strategies. First introduced by Royal Dutch Shell, scenario analyses are the most important tools for the discipline. Intelligently used, they are capable of linking quantitative and qualitative estimates of the alternative futures.

— Better measures of the actual benefits of sound risk management. Arguably, in banking, adoption of new risk management practices may reduce national or regional requirements for minimum capital—a tangible benefit—but are there other quantitative benefits we can use to show the importance of the tools of risk management?

— Systems for on-going, two-way dialogues with critical stakeholder groups and interested parties. Few, if any, organizations I know now use intelligent risk communication mechanisms with key stakeholders, altering their strategies accordingly. The Internet gives us that opportunity. Can we use it wisely?

— Larger and more sophisticated financial reserves for contingencies, available for use for a variety of needs and immediately callable. Will instruments of the capital market replace the inefficient, conflicted, volatile, and financially insecure commercial insurance industry? Do pooled contingency reserves make any sense? Will we inevitably rely more on government and NGO funds, as we did in the Indonesian tsunami, the Pakistani earthquake and US hurricanes? Will we move to pooled pension plans for the private sector following the example of TIAA/CREF in the United States, as this country faces its problems with both the public social security system and private corporate plans?

— Behavioral economics will predict how humans respond to various contingencies. Neuro-scientists now see "a great overlap between the brain's reward-seeking and loss-aversion circuits." (See Gardiner Morse, "Decisions and Desire," *Harvard Business Review,* January 2006). The desire for reward creates as many bad decisions as the desire to avoid loss! That is another reason to combine decision-making for both favorable and unfavorable contingencies.

— Use of genetic signals in human beings for organizational roles. Amy Harmon (in *The New York Times,* June 15, 2006, in "That Wild Streak—Maybe It Runs in the Family") suggests we may use genetic markers to help to find the right jobs for the right people. Should a risk officer be inherently a risk taker or a risk avoider? Rather than select CROs because of their backgrounds in mathematics, market trading, actuarial science or insurance, perhaps we will review their genetic makeup to find the right balance.

We will find new tools, but will they be better?

From astrology to phrenology to risk management, we still search for better ways to explore and prepare ourselves for possible futures. Every decision involves uncertainty. Some uncertainty can be translated into risk, based on information and experience. Assessing and responding to that risk more intelligently is the goal of risk management. Doubt and curiosity remain our touchstones. It promises to be an interesting future!

I conclude with a haiku I first quoted in 1982, from the Japanese poet Basho. It is as pertinent now as then.

A thicket of summer grass
Is all that remains
Of the dreams and ambitions
Of ancient warriors.

APPENDIX 1

A Risk Management Reading List

Periodically throughout my years as editor and publisher of *Risk Management Reports,* I've suggested a selection of those books that, I think, belong in the library of any student of the discipline. This is my reading list, updated to late 2007. It is thoroughly *personal*, based on my own reading and interests, and it is always in flux. I'm sure that others can and will take issue with some selections as well as add their own. This list, which started out as my "ten best," has inevitably expanded to the "top eighteen," because of the need to cover history and philosophy as well as the significant offerings in finance, public policy and other risk specialties. One was written in 1921 and the latest came out in 2007.

Here are my selections:

- Peter Bernstein, *Against the Gods: The Remarkable Story of Risk,* John Wiley & Sons, New York (1997): Peter's "epic" easily tops my list in terms of value, perspective, and prose quality.
- Nassim Nicholas Taleb, *The Black Swan: The Impact of the Highly Improbable,* Random House, New York (2007): a caution on the fragility of knowledge and the limitations of experience and learning. Uncertainty prevails and the unexpected *will* occur.
- Billy Vaughn Koen, *Discussion of the Method,* Oxford University Press, Oxford (2003): This is an engineer's challenging dissertation on dealing with uncertainty through the use of continually-updated "heuristics," or rules-of-thumb.
- Frank Knight, *Risk, Uncertainty and Profit,* University of Chicago Press, Chicago (1921), reissued by Harper & Row, New York (1965): This remains the "classic" introduction to the subject.
- John Adams, *Risk,* UCL Press, London (1995): John's dissection of risk and its management is a pertinent and thoughtful work of art.
- Peter Schwartz, *The Art of the Long View,* Doubleday, New York (1991): The classic introduction to scenario analysis, from an architect of its use at Royal Dutch Shell.

- Richard P. Feynman, *The Pleasures of Finding Things Out,* Perseus Books, Cambridge, Massachusetts (1999): Profound wisdom on the nature of uncertainty, the importance of continuing doubt, the limitations of the scientific method and the glory of "muddling through."
- Vernon Grose, *Managing Risk: Systematic Loss Prevention for Executives,* Prentice-Hall, New York (1986): An aeronautical engineer's practical introduction to the risk management process.
- David McNamee and Georges Selim, *Risk Management: Changing the Internal Auditor's Paradigm,* Institute of Internal Auditors, Altamonte Springs, Florida (1998): A fresh view of the process from the internal audit profession.
- Vlasta Molak, Editor, *Fundamentals of Risk Analysis and Risk Management,* CRC Press, Boca Raton, Florida (1997): The essentials from the view of public policy practitioners.
- James Lam, *Enterprise Risk Management,* John Wiley & Sons, New York (2003): An expression of the expansion of the discipline throughout an organization, as written by the first Chief Risk Officer.
- Michel Crouhy, Dan Galai and Robert Mark, *The Essentials of Risk Management,* McGraw-Hill, New York (2006): A second, updated edition incorporating the essence of financial risk management.
- Robert J. Shiller, *Irrational Exuberance,* Broadway Books, New York (2000): An introduction to some of the behavioral aspects of what we do.
- William Leiss, *In the Chamber of Risks: Understanding Risk Controversies,* McGill-Queen's University Press, Montreal (2001): An essential book on risk communications, its promises and pitfalls.
- Michael Power, *Organized Uncertainty: Designing a World of Risk Management,* Oxford University Press, Oxford (2007: A sweeping analysis of the entire history and nature of risk management.
- George Head and Melanie Herman, *Enlightened Risk Taking,* Nonprofit Risk Management Center, Washington, DC (2002): One of the best, clearest and most concise statements of the process, intended for nonprofits but applicable to all organizations.
- Edward Tenner, *Why Things Bite Back: Technology and the Revenge of Unintended Consequences,* Vintage Books, New York (1996): A constant reminder than what we plan inevitably results in "unintended consequences."
- John F. Ross, *The Polar Bear Strategy,* Perseus Books, Reading, Massachusetts (1999): A primer on our continuing inability to deal with risk rationally.

And finally, I add the timeless book, essential for anyone using English as the primary means of written and oral communication:

- William Strunk, Jr. and E. B. White, *The Elements of Style,* Macmillan Publishing Co., New York (1979)

Do I understand everything in these learned volumes? Hardly, but I have learned more about the nature of risk and our attempts to come to grips with it. With some second and third readings, with their use as references, and with my own evolving experience, I have found fresh insights (and occasional disagreements).

Good reading!

For me to cease writing would not be a rest, it would be a deprivation.

Robertson Davies, *A Merry Heart,* McClelland & Stewart, Toronto, 1996